CULTURE YOUR CULTURE

Innovating Experiences @Work

CULTURE YOUR CULTURE

Innovating Experiences @Work

BY

KAREN JAW-MADSON
Co.- Design of Work Experience, USA

United Kingdom — North America — Japan — India — Malaysia — China

Emerald Publishing Limited
Howard House, Wagon Lane, Bingley, BD16 1WA, UK

British Library Cataloguing in Publication Data
A catalogue record for this book is available from the British Library

ISBN: 978-1-78743-899-6 (Print)
ISBN: 978-1-78743-898-9 (Online)
ISBN: 978-1-78754-501-4 (Epub)

ISOQAR certified
Management System,
awarded to Emerald
for adherence to
Environmental
standard
ISO 14001:2004.

Certificate Number 1985
ISO 14001

INVESTOR IN PEOPLE

CONTENTS

LIST OF FIGURES

Role of Leadership   28

ACKNOWLEDGMENTS

"Thank God."

This phrase comes up in conversation quite often. The thing about common colloquialisms is that they sometimes lose meaning, and as a result, impact. And yet when it came to sitting down and writing my acknowledgments, "Thank God" was the first thing that came to mind. It speaks volumes for how I feel. This book played a part in my greater personal, spiritual, and professional journey over the last few years. By 2013, climbing up the corporate ladder left me unhealthy in body and spirit. I was burned out and wondered where my pursuit of an inspired, thriving life went astray. Over the course of time, I made a commitment to take better care of myself. The aim: to focus on work where I could truly find passion, make a difference, and personally grow. A folder on my computer is named "My New Life" and indeed it is.

At the tail end of this book project, my life (and my heart) expanded even more with the arrival of my son, who was aptly named Christian Hong-Ji. I am amazed at the abundance of good things that matter most. They exist in spite of the crazy world we share and the unique set of struggles each one of us are challenged to overcome. I hope to never lose sight of that fact.

So when I say "Thank God," I am referring to first and foremost my profound gratefulness for the many blessings in my life that afforded me the opportunity to write this book and survive working independently. Were it not for my faith, my family, my friends, and colleagues along the way, I would not be where I am today. I truly could not have done this on my own. There are many to thank, especially Jesus Christ my savior, my parents Paul and Amy, best-husband-in-the-world Jason, my siblings, Timothy and Christine, and my extended friends and family for your steadfast encouragement and support. Thank you to Dr. Tom Keller, my chiropractor in the Midwest and informal life guide. You so patiently saw me through my healing journey with wonderful stories, gentle questions, and chicken soup for both the soul and the body. Ron and Patricia, thank you for giving us our fresh start in CA. Much love to all.

I also have so much gratitude for Emerald, who saw the potential in my proposal – Pete Baker for bringing me in, Eve Hawksworth for getting things going, and Helen Alexander for the dedication and partnership throughout the editorial process. I'd also like to recognize Abi Masha and Sujatha Subramaniane for your partnership and hard work during the final edits of this manuscript. Thank you Dr. dt ogilvie for introducing me to my publisher in the first place. Eric Rayman, how glad I am to have met you through Timothy Rogers. Your sage advice on contracts was so invaluable. My appreciation is worth repeating for my husband Jason Madson, this book's very first editor and greatest cheerleader, and my sister, Christine Usmen, a busy working mom, for reading, editing, and providing your opinions and reactions. Special thanks also to Dr Rochelle Parks-Yancy for your thorough academic review and Annetta Hanna for your willingness to work with me in shaping the manuscript as my developmental editor. Not only were you wonderful to work with, but your coaching made this final version so much better than the first. I built greater confidence and skill under your tutelage.

For your time and willingness to provide stimulating conversation during the writing of this book, I'd like to recognize Len Banks, Becky Bearse, Carol Cherkis, Lawrence Chi, Rick DeVleeschouwer, David Esposito, Hua Han, Beth Kavelaris, Laura McHugh, Rick Moyer, Joe Mulhearn, Patrick O'Brien, Francine Parham, David Perls, Karen Smith, Brian Sorge, Mark Wefler, and Lindsay Wolff Logsdon. Your perspective inspired and kept me from feeling too lonely while writing.

I have many intellectual heroes, some of which were mentioned in this book: Tim Brown, W. Warner Burke, David Cooperrider, Jeanne Liedtka, Roger Martin, and Peter Senge. Many more have encouraged and stimulated this curious mind and fed its learning. This book is my contribution and in appreciation for your pioneering work.

All of you, named here or not, who have been a part of my life and contributed to my experiences, I offer my sincere thanks once again and dedicate this book to you.

Karen Jaw-Madson
Redwood City, CA

INTRODUCTION

Topics covered in this chapter:

• Why and how this book was written and for whom

• The origin of DOWE

> *What would you say about the best and the worst jobs you ever had?*
>
> *What was it about the conditions (people, behaviors, and the environment) that made it so? How did these work situations affect you, your relationships, your productivity, your life?*

When you think about it, the impact of good and bad experiences at work are significant. The best situations don't just feel good – they produce great work. For an employer, multiple factors need to be in place for this to happen consistently for many people, as often as possible. The goal is to align individuals and organizations to interact in the most mutually beneficial ways. Few experience this rare ideal and even then it appears to happen accidentally before it fades away. People spend the rest of their careers looking for it again. Others might say all this sounds lofty, maybe even unrealistic. Since when do agendas line up between employees, their leaders, and the business? This hasn't stopped people from looking for it.

It is possible to increase the chances that this mythical alignment happens. The foundation for connecting the right people in the right job in the right organization in the right environment begins with a great culture manifested in equally great experiences at work. Culture is complex and unique to every organization. It can't be "hacked" nor can it be "bootstrapped" forever. Because of its powerful influence in day-to-day operations, people's lives and ultimately business results, culture should be managed with the same (if not

greater) degree of importance as any other business asset. Many organizations don't take advantage of this opportunity to differentiate themselves.

Organizational culture, experiences at work, and talent can be managed
much like an investment portfolio. You might diversify across sectors, decide
between a growth or value tilt, and make changes over time. You understand
how the different parts come together to meet your present and future goals.
You can maximize your returns if you manage it well. You can also choose
to ignore your investments, but then you have to accept that performance
might never reach its full potential.

This book promises to show you how Design of Work Experience
(DOWE) can enable your organization to systematically build culture and
experiences at work that support the achievement of business strategies — if
you are willing to do your part. It's not intended to be a magic wand. The
answer might be that there is no *one* solution but rather the right *combination* of solutions. With so many choices available, what do you want to do?
DOWE can help you figure it out.

DOWE ORIGINS

As you will discover with DOWE, the journey is as important as the results.
In that spirit, I'd like to share with you how this book came to be. Years
ago, I was fortunate enough to assemble and lead a one-of-a-kind team at a
large multinational corporation. Our mission was to develop a global talent
management strategy with a new approach. Inspired by the recent implementation of a design program, we were asked to experiment with a consumer
product development process and apply it to talent. For the following nine
months, our team was given the freedom to learn and work together as a
"leaderless team" without hierarchies. We conducted extensive user research
to master our understanding of employees' perceptions and needs. We
selected external subject matter experts to provide stimulus. In the end, we
created all the content for a multiyear strategy. Truth be told, the ideas
we presented weren't all that exceptional. What gave it impact can be attributed to the strategy's *relevance* to the organization for which it was created.
That's because it was custom-made for this particular context.

When I saw the degree of engagement from both leadership and employees *throughout* the initiative, I realized something: This was a journey the

organization had to take *with us* in order to be ready for *real* change. No subject matter expert or decision from above could've generated the same enthusiasm. Maybe the opportunity for people to have a say in something that impacted their own lives elicited universal ideals of freedom and liberty. Perhaps it also triggered a phenomenon that's been called the "IKEA effect". the greater the effort invested, the more value placed on the successful completion of one's own creation – something that could be touched and felt *while* it's being developed (Norton, Mochon, & Ariely, 2012). Regardless, taking design as an approach gave life to our process and enlightened all of us with *what could be.* Change begins the moment new possibilities beyond the status quo are considered. I first heard, "our worlds are formed by the questions we ask" while working with David Cooperrider, Professor at Case Western Reserve University's Weatherhead School of Management. If you pause to think about this, it's a little mind-blowing – because it's true.

Throughout my career, I've had responsibility for cultivating the culture, talent, and engagement within many work environments, sometimes in the midst of extraordinary changes. This is what I learned – and I'll put it in performance management terms: how we manage people in the workplace – particularly culture – needs improvement, desperately. Inspired by human-centered design, Design of Work Experience (DOWE) is intended to address this unmet need by giving companies a way to innovate their workplace experiences and maximize the potential in their people.

HOW THIS BOOK WAS BORN

I've led a number of projects since that first initiative – each was an opportunity to combine academic research with the refinement of DOWE as a concept and practice. It wasn't long before I realized I had to share it for the greater good. I wrote this book in the spirit of design: iteratively, in collaboration, and inspired by ideas from other places. I was never formally trained on how to write a book nor was I familiar with the publishing process. I learned by doing, through trial and error, mistakes included. Ideas came from seemingly unrelated and surprising places. I worked in different parts of the manuscript partially and simultaneously, jumping between the big picture and the tiny details, keeping things incomplete for as long as possible.

There were endless iterations as the book went through revision after revision. Sometimes I went analog — off my computer and into quiet contemplation with good old-fashioned pen and paper. Changing routines helped me think differently.

When I got lonely and sluggish, I found new energy talking with others about their perspectives and experiences. Ideas marinated while I did other things, especially when I was stricken with writer's block. On the toughest days, I reassured myself with Anne Lamott's *Bird by Bird* and her advice on "Shitty First Drafts" (Lamott, 1994, pp. 21–27). The writing I did in my first draft, as bad as it was, gave me the chance to try again, improve, and create something better. Writing this book was remarkably more difficult than I ever imagined, partly because it's so important to me and partly because it's really hard work. It demanded persistence, even on days when I had no appetite for it. Still, I had to keep moving forward, going slowly at what felt like a snail's pace when I really just wanted things to go faster. At a certain point, I had to throw away the outline and allow a better version of the book to reveal itself. Bit by bit, what diverged widely slowly came together. Now this finished book is much different (read: better) from what I first envisioned. None of this — from beginning to end — was anything like how I was trained to work. My linear left-to-right modus operandi was ill suited to the creative writing process, so I had to fight through my discomfort in order to experiment and learn new things. My chiropractor's words became an adopted mantra: "Relax and enjoy the folding."

I have two reasons for sharing so many details about the writing of this book. The first is to show how much design has changed my life. It's made such an impact that it transformed the way I think, the way I work, the way I live. It could do that for you too, if you are open to it. The second is to use the writing of this book as a preview for what it will be like to create culture using DOWE: you'll need to be curious, learn through exploration, diverge and converge, practice flexibility, collaborate with others, empathize with multiple perspectives, apply creativity, take opportunities, be iteratively persistent, and — most importantly — *trust the process*. So if you choose DOWE, you will choose all the hard work that comes with it. It will seem chaotic and counterintuitive on the one hand, but also exciting and promising on the other hand. You'll feel both energized and overwhelmed. Time will feel like it's entered a vortex where things appear fast and slow at the same time. The experience will stretch you in ways you have never been stretched, but you will learn a lot and come to see its value.

USING THIS BOOK

This is not your typical business book. I ask that you dismantle your mental models and consider this text on its own merits. Three intertwined, yet distinct spaces are evident: it's part business case, part how-to, and part commentary. In the business case, I present the need for and the merits of DOWE for your consideration. In the how-to, I offer practical and actionable steps for using DOWE in practice, along with advice learned from real-life application. The third space offers perspective and ideas for your rumination. Think of it as parts of the same conversation happening at different times. I'm sure that you'll discover much on your own, and I encourage you to share it as a contribution to our collective knowledge.

Different from other texts, I've kept the inspiring examples and conversations I reference as anonymous as possible: who said what isn't really the point so much as *what was said*. At least in this circumstance, the source is not what gives credibility – it is the content. That being said, names are occasionally provided to give credit to work done by others and to point you to a direct resource.

You'll also find fewer stories here than some other books you've read, and no chapters dedicated to specific case studies. I'm a big believer in the power of storytelling and evidence-based research. With this book, however, stories had to be carefully selected because DOWE is all about taking your own path to finding your own solutions. To discourage the temptation to simply copy what others have done, the only anecdotes used here are either applicable to all contexts and audiences or analogies to explain ideas. It is my hope that through the practice of DOWE, you will create and contribute your own narratives for sharing.

While I would be tickled to have you, the reader, so riveted that you absorb every word in these pages with enthusiasm, this book does not need to be read cover to cover. However, it is important that you get the key parts down – the overview of the concept (Chapter 2) and the how-to (Chapters 4–9). Feel free to otherwise jump around and in between as needed.

If you've gotten this far, this book is for you. It is intended to be a resource for people and organizations using DOWE to apply innovation to culture and to guide its co-creation journey.

Regardless of your role or position, if you care about culture, need change, and are willing to work for it differently, you are invited to join me.

CHAPTER 1

A COMMON NEED

Topics covered in this chapter:

• Today's workplace challenges and the future of work

• The need for new approaches and innovation

> *"It's like a suit jacket that doesn't fit," my coworker said. "No matter how many times I adjust, something just feels off." I understood what she meant, but where was this problem coming from? The company had decent products and values to match — anyone could get behind them. The thing is, the "right fit" has to do with so much more than shared values; it extends to the culture's <u>lived experience</u>. When it feels right, it feels really right, but when it's wrong, <u>everything's</u> wrong.*

Most people think about work experience as achievements you put on your resume. There's also the type of work experience that has to do with "what it's like to work there," the kind that has the potential to either enrich or harm the quality of your life. It's in every employer's best interest to create the good kinds of experiences — the ones that increase job satisfaction, employee engagement, and company performance. Whether your organization is in startup mode or long established, you've got to figure out how to manage your culture and its related experiences — not only for the many benefits it brings, but to avoid the dreaded *or else*. You only need to read the headlines to know how often dysfunctional cultures are blamed for corporate scandals and other disasters. Threats aside, there is a huge opportunity gap between where company cultures are today and our aspirations for

7

them. A 2015 survey from Columbia Business School and Duke University found that out of almost 2,000 CEOs and CFOs, 90% said corporate culture was important, but only 15% felt that their culture was where it needed to be (Columbia Business School, 2015). The follow up question might ask, "What is being done?"

As if doing business wasn't challenging enough, employing people means figuring out how to best utilize, develop, and manage diverse talent in ever-changing circumstances. And it's here – "the future of work" – the one where the boundaries of our collective understanding are being disrupted every day. The concept of work is being redefined. The war for talent rages on. The emergence of the freelancer in the "gig economy" muddles what is internal/external to the company. The lines between nonprofit (or public) and for-profit (or private) are softening. A socially minded business calls itself "not only for profit" (Armstrong, 2014), while another regards their product testers (who are also customers) part of the company and their community (Brodesser-Akner, 2014). Then there's the organization that accepted a visiting executive from another company on a developmental rotation.

How people work is changing as well. The 9–5 schedule is becoming less and less relevant. Many are working on different timetables, longer and shorter, regular and irregular. Co-working centers are now in most major metropolitan cities, from San Francisco to New York. These are the physical workspaces that are shared among multiple startups, small businesses, and solopreneurships to encourage networking or even partnerships. Virtual work arrangements, online team collaboration, and videoconferencing are commonplace. Technology has enabled different ways of working, from the cloud to software as a service to communication tools to productivity applications and beyond.

How knowledge is transmitted and received is also changing. Large, blue chip companies are regularly reaching out externally, using open innovation forums to invite outsiders to co-design new solutions (Das, 2011). Other organizations give away proprietary information to encourage advancement or societal change, like the social networking platform that designated their core software infrastructure as open source ("Thrift: We're Giving Away Code," 2007). Other tech companies have followed suit. A mining company became a well known innovation case study after they publicly shared all their previously confidential geological data and invited participants to help them literally find gold. In the end, they netted \$3B out of a \$575K investment in prize money (Tapscott & Williams, 2007).

Companies are trying out different working paradigms. They buy other businesses, not for products and services, but for their talent. It's known as acqui-hiring (Williams & Perez, 2014). They bring back previous employees they call "boomerang hires" because they left the company and return with even more experience. #FutureofWork is mentioned on social media up to 10,000 times per week, which means people are buzzing about it.

All this indicates that work isn't going to change, *it already has*. With these developments happening at the same time with greater frequency, it may seem like a bunch of moving targets for employers who must juggle talent and culture internally and the future of work externally. How will your organization respond?

THE BEST PRACTICES MYTH

Let's start with what not to do: misuse best practices. When confronting challenges, organizations choose solutions that may have worked elsewhere, but find they only superficially address or temporarily relieve symptoms (Senge, 2006, p. 103). It's a form of hacking – making do, quick and dirty. Emulating best practices is easy; just spend money on trendy amenities, programs, or technology even if they're disconnected from strategy, purpose, or the people they are intended to help. They may set precedents or costs they can't sustain because they lack what's been called a "market-proof culture" (Ruch, 2016).

Best-in-class products and practices may sometimes mask or divert attention from the true nature of the very problems they are attempting to fix. For example, a company decided to install an expensive timekeeping system instead of confronting employees who were abusing policies. UX Designer and author of *The Best Interface is No Interface*, Golden Krishna, would equate this to "slapping an interface on it" (Krishna, 2015). When implemented wholesale, best practices come with mixed results. Instead of being right for everybody, they're a little wrong for most.

Many best practices do, of course, have some validity. The problem is in how they're used. One solution is applied to one problem in isolation. There's a failure to consider the impact of the practice on the whole and to integrate actions. They don't dig beyond the surface to the fundamental needs or root causes. These actions inadvertently cause new problems (Senge, 2006, p. 58) and might not address the old problems either.

Then there's the tendency to emphasize "practice" over resolution: a decision is made. Once it's carried out, the problem is considered solved. The focus then shifts away from the initial problem and more toward the tactics of implementation.

Best practices are great when used appropriately but not when they are counted on as standalone, one-size-fits-all solutions. Besides, how does differentiation happen if everyone is doing the same thing? How about we call for some creativity in our workplace practices?

THE IMPORTANCE OF CONTEXT

Whatever your organizational challenges might be, here's what you can't overlook: an unprecedented, deep understanding of your organization's unique context. The use of that knowledge ensures solutions that are authentic and relevant. *This* is what determines your starting point of "how" – and goes so much farther than your typical surveys and focus groups.

What makes up the context, or what organizational psychologist Peter Senge might refer to as the "system," consists of the following:

Business Factors: Typical business factors include the competitive landscape, regulatory issues, economic and industry pressures, internal and external forces, and so on. These are the circumstances that generate work. Organizational elements such as strategies, policies, mission, and values fall within this sphere because they are your company's challenge to itself to live up to why it exists and how it intends to do business. All the opportunities and issues that require leadership (or are created by leadership) are business factors too.

Culture: Culture is a construct reflected in all things that have the power to influence behaviors, interactions, and perception within a socially defined entity or institution. Examples of what reflects culture include: norms, literal and figurative messages, artifacts, and so on. These work together to determine the boundaries of what is acceptable and not acceptable. They are manifested in how people behave, interact, react, and perceive reality. Culture is created, reinforced, and experienced by people. It includes not just what's said, but what's actually lived. Because components that reflect culture can be modified – particularly behavior – culture can ultimately be changed over time.

---

*NOTE: The term "culture" itself is colloquially used in layman's terms as a catch-all for all things related to the work environment. Scholarly research and commentary on culture is far more nuanced. To learn more, start with Edgar Schein's book, *Organizational Culture and Leadership* (2017).

Environment: These are the conditions set by business factors and the culture. Physical and psychological, tangible and intangible, environment is where interactions and experiences happen. The term "climate" describes an environment's defining characteristics.

Behaviors: Behaviors are the actions people take (or don't take) that either reinforce or clash with the cultural norms and standards. They are what is most accessible and changeable for individuals.

Experiences: All the events, patterns, and dynamics created by the combination of business factors, culture, environment, and behaviors make up "what's it's like" to work somewhere – the experience. Any aspect of life in the organization, including interactions and processes, are the smaller experiences that make up the overall experience.

People: Every company deals with a unique combination of many individuals who have an influence on its organizational life. They serve in different capacities and are the key drivers behind all the other components that make up an organization's context. People really do mean everything to a business.

It would be easy to assume these exist in a hierarchical relationship, with people as the common thread throughout: business factors create the culture, which sets the conditions of the environment, influences behaviors, and determines the outcome(s) as lived experiences (Figure 1.1).

In reality, these elements interact with one another symbiotically, where changes in one area can influence or impact others, directly and indirectly (Figure 1.2).

From the systems thinking perspective, the double arrows in Figure 1.2 represent "feedback" to demonstrate how actions can reinforce or counteract each other, ultimately changing the overall context (Senge, 2006, p. 73).

Figure 1.1. Context as a Hierarchy.

Figure 1.2. Context as a System.

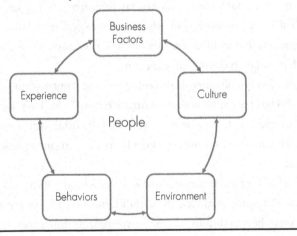

There are those that believe that you can't change culture directly. Technically, that's true. Because everything's interconnected, it's not that simple and finite. It's possible to directly influence and change the behaviors, environment, and experiences in an organization to the degree that the culture is ultimately transformed. The connectedness of the system is also why it's more prudent to consider culture strategically. Attempting to change just one aspect will have chain reactions that will require broader management regardless. It's better to be prepared and manage it holistically.

Another way of looking at the workplace would be to examine the enterprise in terms of scale: at the individual, team, and organization levels. Try to complete the table in Figure 1.3. How are these aspects of organizational life experienced at the individual, team, and organizational levels? To what degree are they consistent or incongruent with each other?

Figure 1.3. Context by Scale.

	Individual	Team	Organization
Business Factors			
Culture			
Environment			
Behaviors			
Experience			

Where there's the tendency to consider things in opposition to one another (i.e. Organizational vs. Individual needs), this table provides a view on how each component fits and interacts with the whole. To illustrate, the individual is a standalone person, a member of a team, and part of the organization – all at the same time. This is a more accurate reflection of the reality.

Every workplace has its own unique context made up of business factors, culture, environment, behaviors, experiences, and people. These determine how talent strategies and solutions apply, for better or worse.

A COMMON NEED

Here's the context we all share: creating and managing great cultures is challenging, and it's all being done in dynamic markets where the definition of work is changing. Meanwhile, organizations are attempting to tap into the full potential of their talent – or they should be. Everyone knows that employee mindsets have a direct relationship to engagement, productivity, performance, and ultimately, profitability and growth. Setting the conditions – purposefully managing the surrounding circumstances for the better – is not only good for business, it's good for people.

We are social creatures, and our interactions have the capacity to be either beneficial or harmful to us. Scientific research has shown the direct impact of our relationships on our overall well-being – not just psychologically, but biologically as well. To paraphrase Dr. Thomas Lewis, professor at UCSF and neuroscientist: relationships are physical, living, biological processes between people all the time, every day. Like owning a plant, if you water it only once a month, it will die (Lewis, 2015). The effects of our relationships and experiences at work are neither intangible nor unimportant, as they too often are mistaken to be. Given the amount of time we spend working, a critical opportunity exists for organizations to maximize and harness the benefits of interactions.

Furthermore, to remain competitive, companies *have to* differentiate themselves through meaningful work experiences and motivating environments that are customized to their unique context. One of the top retailers in the world (per square foot sales) knows that "...if you're not reinventing your experience every five years, you're behind the curve...it's not a great position to be in, where the competition just sucks more than you do" (Chu, 2014). Any organization that wants to be the best has to set its standards not in relation to others, but in accordance to its highest aspirations.

Another company was blindsided one year when they fell off one of the "Top Companies" lists. While they continued to maintain their practices year over year, they were unaware that other companies made even greater efforts and surpassed them. Lesson learned: even those basking in success should plan for and manage disruption of the status quo. They should do this regularly in order to prepare for the inevitability of change – or better yet, manage it in *real time, all the time*.

If an organization neglects to manage themselves, it will be done for them. One such company took this to heart, taking bold steps in changing the way they do business in order to continue to lead in their industry. In speaking with one of their leaders, it's evident why they were willing to do this. Failure to act and becoming a has-been headline is feared far more than failing at innovation.

Employment is like a sweatshirt. Sweatshirts have been around for decades, readily available and highly commoditized as a wardrobe staple. Everyone knows what to expect with sweatshirts because they've been that way for a long time. Along came an entrepreneur who decided to redesign the sweatshirt from scratch, down to the most minute detail (Manjoo, 2012). Consumers responded, buying up all the inventory to the point where the manufacturer couldn't keep up with demand. Other sweatshirt manufacturers are likely paying attention, perhaps thinking about how they should respond with their own products. It's this type of thinking that's needed if we are to replace long-established patterns with new possibilities. The evolution of work is already in motion, and employers know they must be competitive. To do this, they need to learn how to innovate work experiences.

CHAPTER 2

ENTER DOWE

Topics covered in this chapter:

- Innovation and design as the basis of DOWE

- Definition of DOWE and its process, mindset, and behaviors

- Role of leadership

- Caveats and clarifications.

FROM DESIGN TO DOWE

Innovation doesn't come from the technological discoveries and advancements themselves, but from a phenomenon that occurs when ingenuity meaningfully links to a critical mass of people. In other words, invention becomes innovation when it makes a difference in people's lives.

Design and innovation are often part of the same discussion. As taught at Rotman School of Design, "Design is the process of making or *doing* something new. And that's where design is more aligned with innovation on a grand scale: it is not an *attribute*, it is fundamentally about *action*" (Fraser, 2013). Others take it even further, saying "Innovation is Design and Design is Innovation" (Epperson, 2013).

If you type "definition of design" into a search engine, it is generally described as the intentional meaning, concepts, or ideas that form the basis of something created. Implied in all things design is the concept of connection – between the design, what's created, and its audience – a

connection or connections that elicit some sort of response, behavior, or outcome. Designers have long been able to connect with their audiences in compelling ways. The most obvious examples are found in physical objects or
structures, such as the way Frank Lloyd Wright lowered ceilings as a subcon-
scious cue to sit down. Or consider how wheelchair accessible stairs in
Figure 2.1 marry function and form at the same time, providing an elegant
way for both the disabled and able-bodied to move from one level to
another.

The recognition that design could address a range of human needs –
from art to product development to services and experiences – has opened
up new possibilities for innovation. Think of how the market for mp3
players transformed into a platform for enjoying music *as an experience*.
Even that's changed. These days, it is all about combining intelligence with
streaming radio to accommodate changing tastes and consumer behavior.

Design has found applicability anywhere from business to education to
social causes and community building, bringing forth new and different
experiences. Though it offers us powerful tools and methodologies, design's
greatest gift is its mindset. Design encourages the ability to creatively

**Figure 2.1. McGaugh Hall, UC Irvine, Designed by Architect Arthur
Erickson.**

synthesize solutions that are based on a deep, empathetic understanding of people and their needs. This is "design thinking" – the thought process by which a design is formed. Good design doesn't happen without design thinking.

Companies already recognize the importance of knowing people – their customers. They spend an estimated $6.7 billion in the United States, and up to $18.9 billion worldwide on market research to delve into the lives of their target audience (Anderson, 2010). What's learned is applied to designing experiences that win business and build brands. In product design, research might include a visit with a stay-at-home dad who describes or demonstrates certain activities and/or uses of products. Other researchers might review videos created by people talking about their favorite hobbies or their recent purchases. These activities generate a ton of data ready for insights on how consumers think, feel, and choose, what they like and don't like, how they are motivated, and so on. Designers synthesize data into knowledge, and knowledge into great products and appealing experiences.

Recall what it's like to go to a store and buy a computer. What happens when you walk in the door? What do you see? How are things arranged? What kinds of interactions do you encounter? What do you pass by, and where do you linger? You'll realize that this is more than a mere purchase transaction. You are in fact going through a purposefully designed experience that is familiar to you and very distinctive of that brand. If implemented as intended, a well-designed experience aligns the interests of people and business. It's a win-win. When it's off, it's blatantly obvious because it generates negative reactions. That's the power of good and bad design – there's a cause and effect no matter what.

Imagine if companies turned that same focus and attention inward toward their own employees. What if all organizations knew and valued their employees as much as their customers? This is not a new notion. Bernd Schmitt, Columbia Business School professor specializing in marketing and customer experience, refers to employees as internal customers who should be directly involved with the business' brand (Schmitt, 2010, p. 206). "Employee experience" is an internal resource as part of his complete Customer Experience Management model (Schmitt, 2010, p. 208). A well-known CEO took it one step further, saying, "Everyone talks about building a relationship with your customer. I think you build one with your employees first" (Leahey, 2012). In recent years, companies have created roles that serve the same function, but go by a number of names: employee experience management, community happiness, people and culture, to name a few. Many organizations could stand to have a more meaningful relationship with their employees whether or not these departments exist.

At The Darden School of Business at the University of Virginia, Jeanne Liedtka's Design Thinking for Business Innovation course discusses a set of questions to determine what "problems" are appropriate for design thinking. They include: Is the problem human-centered? How clearly do you understand the problem itself? What's the level of uncertainty? What information is already available to you? If the answer is that:

1. a deep understanding of people is needed to

2. explore and get agreement on the problem while

3. having a high degree of uncertainty and

4. little existing relevant data on which to begin, *then design thinking is appropriate* (Liedtka, 2013).

What better place to apply design thinking than to innovate experiences at work? Imagine a workplace that leverages and enhances its strengths while seeking the satisfaction of unmet needs. How might behaviors, experiences, policies, practices, workspaces, and processes be redesigned as human-centered solutions? What could come out of it? All factors that determine work satisfaction can be purposefully designed — everything that makes up what it's like to work somewhere. This is the Design of Work Experience (DOWE).

WHAT IS DOWE?

DOWE (pronounced ['dü 'wē]) partners employees with their employers to co-create customized and meaningful work experiences that set the conditions for people and business to thrive. It questions current paradigms and introduces new thinking, beginning with the notion that people can become experts at creating their own culture through experiences. Like innovation (Keeley, Walters, Pikkel, & Quinn, 2013, p. 8), like design (Pink, 2005, p. 75), DOWE is open to all. Anyone can be a "DOWE-R" (pronounced "doer"). You don't have to be a trained designer or a subject matter expert.

As consumers of the work experience, everyone is prequalified to contribute. DOWE is neither top-down nor bottom-up, but rather a collaboration of "us with them" (as it is in design), forging a new and different kind of relationship (Brown, 2009, p. 58) between employees and their employers.

The new relationship begins by collaborating on co-creation. A well-known practice in open innovation, co-creation happens when companies bring together different groups of people to solve problems or come up with new solutions. This type of interaction also exists in other arenas, from lean manufacturing to tech hackathons to art and music collaborations. Co-creation engages and builds a collective intelligence that comes from using the creativity, capabilities, and resourcefulness everyone brings to complex challenges (Conklin, 2006, as cited in Benson & Dresdow, 2013). What is co-created is co-owned by the business (represented by its leaders) and its employees. Said one VP who experienced DOWE: "…we are changing our culture. By 'we' I mean the entire group – everyone from the President to the maintenance staff." DOWE brings this innovation practice into workplace culture, where everyone can be a co-creator.

Unlike other organizational concepts, DOWE's main focus is not to solve problems, but to make them obsolete. The contrast between these mindsets is best explained by an example: It started with a manager being called into Human Resources. A recent mass exodus from their department and a rise in employee complaints triggered an investigation. As HR reviewed the key themes, the manager began to take copious notes, creating a list of problems to be addressed. Eventually, the manager was asked, "Think of a time when the department was at its best. If you were able to recreate that, would these problems on your list even matter?" The answer was no. Had the manager addressed items from that list one by one, they would never be finished. What's worse, that tactic would likely lead to a new set of problems before long. It would be a losing battle. However, if the manager enlisted his/her team to make it the best department ever, positive change would be tangible and longer lasting.

There are different ways strengths can be leveraged. Consider existing organizational capability as a strength. For instance, a company good at marketing can use that capability to improve internal communications, branding people programs the same way they do their products. Strengths can also come in the form of people – the few subject matter experts who can be tapped to teach others and to spread their expertise, such as the ability to innovate or work strategically. Strengths can also be characteristics selected for greater emphasis, like how a place that works well during crises can perform at peak levels everyday, minus the stress. DOWE creates the forum by which strengths can be surfaced and integrated as part of solutions.

DOWE also addresses organizational tensions, contradictions, and para-doxes (Putnam, Myers, & Gailliard, 2013). Some examples of where it can be applied include organizations that:

• sell great products, but have unhappy workforces

• enjoy a reputation for having a great culture on the outside, but feel awful on the inside

• are successful in spite of themselves, just waiting to decline

• have organization charts and structures that don't make sense

• espouse one thing, but do another

• suffer with leaders or functions that don't work together

The versatility of DOWE also distinguishes it from other concepts. It can be used to design any experience at work in any industry or initiative of any size and covers a range of circumstances from simple to complex. It also has the flexibility to dovetail with other organizational practices. It does not require strict adherence to rules. Rather, sticking with its principles ensures its effectiveness while also giving room for adjustments. A small team or department can improve or completely redesign the way they work. A start-up's culture can begin with healthy dynamics on the founding team and pur-posefully scale up through rapid growth without losing touch or alignment with its vision. Disparate and siloed programs can be integrated into one cohesive people strategy aligned with business objectives. An entire organiza-tion can be enabled by DOWE to build fundamentals, such as the design and establishment of a new culture, or the creation and realization of vision, mission, and values. Once established, DOWE can help design strategies, practices, and experiences that reflect these foundations and adapt the orga-nization to a changing world. DOWE further advances successful companies to greater levels of maturity and achievement that can only be attained through their people. Turnarounds or adversities can be converted into

Instead of telling FR's to make sure they tell mbrs they are INTGD w/s FR, I should have asked them what they could do to know they are INTGD FR assure that mbrs

DOWE opportunities. The possibilities are limitless. For more ideas, see Chapter 10.

DOWE's designed solutions are unique, curated combinations of elements relevant to an equally unique context. As people begin to thrive at work, they unleash the untapped potential and possibilities often hidden in every organization. Business alignment, differentiation, performance, and success follow. In the way design has transformed and/or created entire markets, it can redefine ways of work. Even better, it can do so on your terms. DOWE develops intimacy and understanding between employer and employee, giving both a say. Because the organization and its employees are partners, they are equally empowered and responsible for the outcomes. With this setup, they are able to work together in unprecedented ways on any organizational challenge. The prospects are exciting.

THE DOWE PROCESS

There's the concept of DOWE and then there's the process of DOWE. "Doing DOWE" means that you have a *new* mindset and a *new* way to design and implement *new* solutions. If you want different results, you have to try different things. DOWE upends the expectation that we must have the (often flawed) answer(s) up front. It begins with a thorough exploration of the context and an open-mindedness to defer decisions in favor of *discovering* the answers through the process instead.

At the macro level, the DOWE process (Figure 2.2) organizes and structures this complex work into four major components: the combination of

Figure 2.2. DOWE Process Overview.

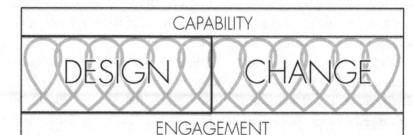

DESIGN and CHANGE enabled by CAPABILITY and ENGAGEMENT. DESIGN is like many design processes across industries – there's the exploration, understanding, designing, and executing. It's followed up with a change management process: the diagnosis, planning, execution, and evaluation.

DESIGN and CHANGE make a great combination. Without CHANGE, what comes out of DESIGN may never be fully realized. It operationalizes the new experience and makes it happen. At the same time, DESIGN gives substance to CHANGE, making it meaningful and profound. Change – like culture – is constant, so it's a matter of whether you manage it purposefully or let change manage you. On their own, they both fall short. Together, they achieve exponentially more than what's been done before. All organizations practicing DOWE must manage a degree of change, for there is inevitably some distance between where you are and where you want to go.

CAPABILITY allows the organization to capitalize on its strengths and develop the skills and abilities needed to achieve a designed outcome. ENGAGEMENT on a widespread basis – top-down, bottom-up, back-and-forth, and in-between – breaks down silos and barriers, replacing them with an integrated community of committed people driving change and performing.

Under these main components, DOWE is organized as a series of iterative learning loops, each with its own specific set of activities that reflect the non-linear, but progressive nature of the process. Ultimately, the model yields an in-depth understanding of the current state, a design for the future state, and a roadmap with action plans for how to get there.

Figure 2.3 details the activities, which will be explained in greater detail with the forthcoming chapters. The transition, or "handoff" (so to speak) from DESIGN to CHANGE occurs during the PLAN phase.

The process concludes with the *Sustain* learning loop, which continues until the context changes and a new round of DOWE is necessary. When that happens, the organization's starting point will be that much more advanced as a result of the previous work.

DOWE creates opportunities for organizations to thoughtfully consider strategic questions before settling on answers. It tempers the urge to quickly identify solutions and immediately execute without full understanding of the context and without planning that takes into account how it's received. Alignment is created between a business and its people by co-creation, drawing boundaries and setting expectations together while providing much needed

Figure 2.3. DOWE Process (Detailed View).

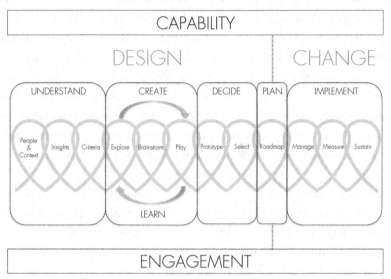

clarity. Most importantly, DOWE keeps the focus in the right place: on people and getting them inspired.

BEHAVIORS AND THE PRACTICE OF DOWE

Though there are different roles to play, all the people of the organization have an opportunity to be involved in the DOWE process. Executive sponsors of the DOWE initiative are expected to not only support, but also participate. Employees provide perspective on the current experience and inspire ideas for the future state through their engagement. A core design team, made up of a diverse cross-section of the company, leads the process on behalf of the organization. The benefit of having this team is to build the capability to design and manage culture from within. DOWE's success depends on the contribution of all these players.

Having the team facilitate the process like a series of tasks is not enough; they have to embody and demonstrate its ideals in action. Together with their sponsors, they must be willing to grapple with the complexities revealed through the process, model the desired future state, and use the mindset and behaviors defined in the practice of DOWE. These include demonstrating the ability to learn, the use of progressive iteration, empathy, forging connections, and skillful agility throughout the entirety of the work.

Everything about doing DOWE is about learning, not just in attaining knowledge and applying it, but also because it calls for the use of different learning styles. Just like in design, it is "an exploratory approach to problem solving that includes and balances both analytical and creative thought processes" (Prud'homme van Reine, 2017, p. 61). Learning also precipitates change — learning to practice new capabilities, learning new behaviors, learning about people's experiences, learning the nuances of how the organization functions, and so on. With each new learning, people change — and if done collectively, the organization transforms.

DOWE learns and acts through iteration. Touted by visionaries such as W. Edwards Deming (O'Toole, 1995, p. 192), iteration is the cyclical loop required for continuous learning and improvement. It is purposefully designed into the process to push DOWE-Rs to go beyond the first answer (which isn't always the right or the best one) and to identify the best solutions through generative reflection and learning (von Oech, 2008, pp. 33—48). It works against people's tendencies to take shortcuts, converge too quickly, and to predefine answers rather than letting the solutions reveal themselves. Where others consume the whole and miss key points, iteration simplifies complexity through a conscientious exploration of interconnected pieces. Instead of risking everything with a — or even one — big decision, iteration allows for smaller decisions along the way, minimizing risk (Brown, 2009, p. 4). DOWE iterates progressively. By extension, the organization learns, evolves, and validates toward the new experience and desired future.

Empathy is the ability to understand and see things as others experience them, moving from self-centeredness to other-centeredness. This is demonstrated by a commitment to honor a collective point of view as opposed to only one's own. Empathy is not only an act of kindness and generosity, but also indispensable to knowing *People & Context* in the DOWE process. The degree to which one can understand and empathize with people determines the ability to design on their behalf. Theresa Wiseman of the Bloomsbury and Islington College of Nursing and Midwifery studied empathy in a field where it's critical — in patient care. She identified these defining attributes: the ability to see the world as others see it, to be nonjudgmental, to understand another's feelings, and communicate the understanding (Wiseman, 1996, p. 1166). Brené Brown, social work scholar and popular Ted Talk speaker, further distinguished empathy from sympathy, noting that empathy is about *connecting* (RSA, 2013).

Doing DOWE connects much more than people to each other, but it also connects people to their organization, needs to solutions, and ideas to reality – just as designers do. This is accomplished through collaboration and follow-through. To create and strengthen connections within an organization like never before, you need to weave a stronger, more connected, more aligned community that works toward mutually shared success.

Agility is the flexibility to shift effectively in a timely fashion, particularly in the face of changing circumstances. Different types of thinking, behaviors, and actions are required throughout the DOWE process, and each has a time and place. Author and consultant Edward De Bono explained this with the analogy of different colored hats (De Bono, 1985). As leaders of the process, DOWE-Rs must be agile enough to switch between "hats," reject overreliance on comfortable hats, and to develop the use of other hats. Being stuck in one hat (as in not being agile) will likewise slow down an organization. By design, DOWE hones one's ability to switch and wear multiple hats – to be agile. DOWE-Rs also exercise agility as they move from seeing the big picture (dilation) to diving into details beneath the surface (constriction) – sometimes simultaneously – to decipher relationships between the individual and the organization (or system) (Bannister, 1962, p. 110). The knowledge gained from this integrated, holistic view informs the design and makes experiences extraordinary. Agility is again called upon during the implementation of change, where moving parts can sometimes lead to unpredictable results. Being able to shift or respond capably can make or break a DOWE initiative.

Learning, iterating, empathizing, connecting, and practicing agility are no small requirements to ask of people, but the rewards can be tremendous. New skills and enlightened perspectives are developed. A personal satisfaction of being part of something bigger, being in the position where one can directly and positively influence an organization and impact the lives of many people is a great value proposition. DOWE-Rs become experts because they possess a depth of understanding that only design can bring. They champion the changes that come with the design and see to it that the organization delivers on its commitments. Best of all, they are the first to thrive in the new experiences they helped to create. DOWE nurtures ownership through co-creation. Those involved are invested in its outcomes and derive great satisfaction from seeing real change happen. One DOWE-R, now retired, called this time the most engaged he ever was in his entire career, and it showed. He was affectionately observed as "getting fired up" over and over again, so much so that his retirement gift was a tabletop fireplace.

ROLE OF LEADERSHIP

Not surprisingly, leadership plays an influential role in the success of DOWE. To begin with, the process calls upon leadership from all involved, regardless of official job title or level. Demonstrating *observable* leader behaviors and skills, such as the courage to envision different possibilities, willingness to learn new things, active participation, and guidance to others throughout change, lends credibility and encourages everyone to be more receptive to the DOWE cause. To boot, co-design brings leaders *closer* to their employees. You, as a leader, must lead in order for DOWE to work and to inspire others to do the same without imposing your will (O'Toole, 1995, p. 254). This doesn't necessarily require all leaders to be inspirational, for there are many kinds of leaders and different leadership styles. Leaders are simply obligated to take action that enables people to become inspired – *as an outcome.*

Leaders tend to set the organization's cultural vision, tone, and direction to such a degree that characteristics of their personalities sometimes become organizational working norms (for better or worse). They have control over "how we do things here" through the power that comes with their position. Therefore, they must be the first role models of the new experiences, for people are watching. Employees will trust and follow a reputable leader even if missteps are made or details aren't figured out (anonymous, personal communication, February 27, 2015). Leaders prove they are trustworthy through their involvement, financial and moral support, and their own actions and behaviors. Ultimately, leaders must play their part in making the culture so clear and so strong that it outlives its creators.

If they exist in the structure of your organization, managers are also critical to the success of DOWE. Though there are differences between these roles, leaders should ideally be good managers, and managers should display leadership qualities. Managers' proximity to employees means that they can greatly influence daily life at work. Their job is to set expectations by example, provide support, coaching, and feedback, and champion commit-ments. These responsibilities are also required to support the change DOWE brings, especially in helping employees and holding them to their own pro-mises. Managers do this through accountability, not blame. According to Brené Brown, "Blame is simply discharging a discomfort and pain. It has an inverse relationship with accountability (RSA, 2015)." This is one of many important distinctions in how DOWE is done. Practicing accountability is about setting expectations and holding people to them – not about assigning fault. Provide positive reinforcement when people deliver on their promises and raise concern and reiterate expectations when they don't.

This goes for informal leaders as well, those that lead by virtue of their work or their capabilities. Anyone who has influence with others, especially change agents, has a role to play in making DOWE a success. But the onus to change *begins* with leaders and managers. Any failure to do their part leads to cultural issues of their own making.

CAVEATS AND CLARIFICATIONS

Note that like innovation and like design thinking, you learn DOWE by doing. Everything you read in this book is conceptual until you live the jour-ney and make it real in your organization. Also, as with design, there is no single way to do DOWE. This book provides intent, rationale, the frame-work, and advice as guiding points. It will also cover what is variable and what is necessary for success. Remember that showing DOWE in action, through collaboration, is far more effective than trying to explain it. As attributed to Benjamin Franklin, "Tell me and I forget, teach me and I may remember, involve me and I learn."

Additionally, DOWE only works for institutions that genuinely see cul-ture and people as key to their business. It is nearly impossible to convince your organization to pursue the purposeful creation of meaningful work experiences if they don't acknowledge that they really need it *and* have the desire to act upon it. Inspiration must come from within your organization, not this book. Furthermore, the organizations that get the most benefit out of DOWE are those whose aim is to be the *best* possible version of what they can be – not just better or different – those with ambitious, Big, Hairy

Audacious Goals (BHAGs), those that aim high to achieve more (Collins & Porras, 1996, p. 73).

DOWE can help organizations to establish or renew their mission and values, align work experiences to match and reflect those values, and advance greater levels of maturity and achievement from there. This concept is values-based and expects values-based leadership for effective change management (O'Toole, 1995, p. 254). That means no matter what happens, whatever situations present themselves, people will act in accordance to their organizational values.

DOWE can therefore never serve as justification for creating work environments based on the personal preferences of the organization's leaders and can never serve to excuse poor behavior or a lack of ethics. To illustrate, passion may be defined as a company's desirable trait but it can never be used to justify yelling at colleagues – that version of "passion" is never acceptable in any workplace. Consider also the design of a culture where jerks succeed. The environment would be relevant and meet the needs of those jerks, but DOWE is meant to create environments where people – good people – thrive. There are boundaries (or rather, inherent values) embedded within DOWE.

Most importantly, DOWE requires fortitude – the courage and tenacity to forge new paths for your organization, to change paradigms, to work through complexity, and to progressively iterate with persistence. All it takes is a brave few who genuinely want change and will work hard for it while using a new approach. Bottom line, DOWE innovates – but only if you let it.

CHAPTER 3

DOWE DECONSTRUCTED

Topics covered in this chapter:

• Conceptual foundations of DOWE

• Underlying principles and rationale behind approach and methodology

• Debating DOWE

Before we get into the "how" of DOWE, it's important to understand the foundation on which it stands. Design of Work Experience comes from what is known about people at work, developed from well over a century of research. Collectively, we learned our way toward this knowledge, and we will inevitably evolve from here as well. As a distinct multidisciplinary concept, DOWE has its own principles, approach, methodology, and is – like anything else – subject to critical analysis. With that said, let's explore DOWE in depth.

A MULTIDISCIPLINARY NETWORK

Design is both multidisciplinary and interdisciplinary, which means it uses and cuts across multiple disciplines. By extension, so does DOWE. Work culture, like other challenging, complex opportunities in business, calls for an integrative approach (Madsbjerg & Rasmussen, 2014, p. 13). DOWE brings together old and new knowledge about people at work from great thinkers, scholars, and scientists – validated across various disciplines. It translates seemingly unrelated concepts from other fields and repurposes them for the creation of work experiences, some of which are discussed in this chapter.

If prevalence and agreement across these many fields are any indication, there are strong arguments for how and why DOWE works. All of the fields in Figure 3.1 have studied ways to observe or affect human behavior. DOWE incorporates what's been learned into its approach and process. Take co-creation, for instance. The practice has been adopted and studied across design, architecture, anthropology, and even manufacturing. Empowerment to affect one's own life is promoted from psychology to spirituality, all from different vantage points. Like any living and open network, some connections are stronger than others and emphasis varies according to each unique DOWE initiative and point in the process. There is tremendous opportunity to explore these and other ties in greater depth for years to come – not to compare and contrast, but to further connect.

DOWE PRINCIPLES

DOWE's raison d'être is to innovate how organizations uniquely define and manage their way of work to the benefit of their employees and their business. Regardless of what that looks like from place to place, or how its applied, four interconnected principles remain consistent. DOWE actions and outcomes must be purposeful, mindful, meaningful, and inspirational.

Purposeful

Purposeful means both *having* purpose (a reason for existing) and doing things *on* purpose (acting based on defined reasons). Bringing people together to collaborate for a greater purpose is a source of inspiration, meaning, and motivation. Most people can earn a paycheck working elsewhere. Why work at this particular organization? Why is this company's business worthy of people's talents and efforts? Why would this place be ideal for some and not others? How can this company align corporate with personal ambitions?

People have natural inclinations to search for purpose and meaning – in work and in life. Moreover, once they buy into a greater purpose, actions toward achieving it have to make sense, be reasonable, and align with

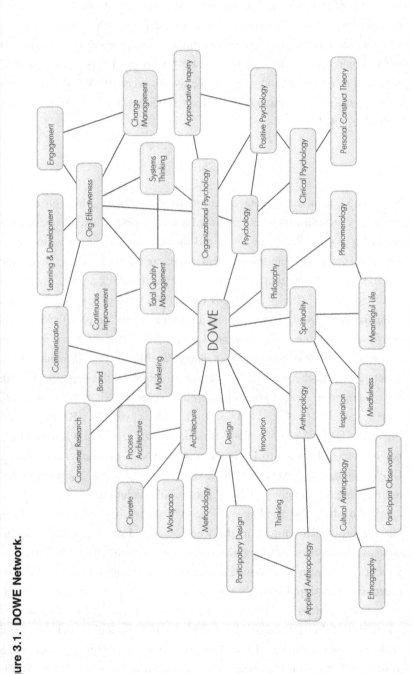

Figure 3.1. DOWE Network.

personal values. For all the streamlining organizations do, lack of purpose is *the source* of common inefficiencies such as bureaucracy, unnecessarily complex processes, work for work's sake, and meetings with no conclusions — all of which are a waste of resources (talent, time, money, sanity). The last thing people want to do is to take action for no good reason, and yet they are asked to do this all too often. To be useful, every DOWE initiative must have a purpose. The answer for why anything is done in DOWE is never "I don't know."

Mindful

Mindfulness is about paying attention to the present. This concept has spread beyond spirituality and into the business world, where companies are beginning to embrace it. Self-aware and forward-thinking organizations benefit from practicing mindfulness and encouraging their people to do the same. They recognize that operating with mindfulness is healthy for people and the business. Clarity and focus come from paying attention to what's immediately in front of us, without judgment, as an "impartial witness to [our] own experience" (Kabat-Zinn, 1991, p. 33). Some refer to it as "being in the now." In the wise words of Paulo Coehlo in *The Alchemist*, "The secret is here in the present. If you pay attention to the present, you can improve upon it. And, if you improve on the present, what comes later will also be better" (Coelho, 1993, p. 108). This is why the DOWE process begins the UNDERSTAND phase with the *People & Context* learning loop before moving forward to DESIGN and CHANGE mindfully. As a result, DOWE designs are relevant to both the present state and the aspirational future, bringing continuity to the organization's evolution.

All too often, the grind toward the ever-elusive future leaves us feeling like the proverbial hamster in the wheel, where distraction often leads to unpleasant surprises. Looking ahead *can* coexist with being mindful in the present, but it must be managed conscientiously. Many respond to the fast-paced world by skipping over important things in rushed judgment, converging quickly to misguided resolutions, arriving at baseless conclusions, or taking thoughtless actions to relieve anxieties, only to double back again and again to repeat mistakes. Paulo Coehlo also wrote, "When you repeat a mistake, it is not a mistake anymore: it is a decision" (Coehlo, 2013). This is the case whether or not awareness is involved. By strictly sticking to the actions of each specific learning loop, DOWE builds mindfulness into its process, making each working moment productive in the present and taking the appropriate amount of time to progress toward its intended outcomes.

Meaningful

People sometimes use these terms interchangeably, but there are distinct differences between the interrelated concepts of happiness and meaning. Happiness is a subjectively defined state of being (Baumeister, Vohs, Aaker, & Garbinsky, 2013, p. 505) that is often short-lived and event-driven. Meaning comes from evaluating life against one's aspirations, for example: purpose, values, and other things of personal significance (Baumeister et al., 2013, p. 506). Happiness and meaning represent different emotive states. Feeling happy can come from a number of things (including what's meaningful), but finding meaning in one's life does not always equate to being happy (Baumeister et al., 2013, p. 506).

At work, the difference between happiness and meaningfulness is distinct. Think about how it feels to receive a promotion versus loving your career, or when people make personal sacrifices to do their job well, prioritizing meaning over happiness (Baumeister et al., 2013, p. 513). A "motivational force" exists where meaning is found (Frankl, 1959, p. 92). That is, we are compelled to both expend and derive energy from things we find meaningful.

As economist E.F. Schumacher wrote in *Good Work*, "...work is the joy of life and is needed for our development, but...meaningless work is an abomination" (Schumacher, 1994, p. 132). What this implies is that having no meaning is even worse than having negative meaning. People can find and interpret meaning anywhere based on their perceptions of good or bad. It is possible – and desirable – to establish a common set of conditions that results in people experiencing meaningful work in a positive way (Bhattacharjee & Mogilner, 2013, p. 2). DOWE provides the framework for organizations to overtly define meaning for themselves and their people. With this degree of transparency, individuals can choose or not choose to be a part of it, and the right people can be matched with the right companies.

Inspirational

The task of an organization is to inspire people as often as possible, because inspired people are engaged people who are energized and focused on their work (Xanthopoulou & Bakker, 2013, p. 25). Better said, inspiration *causes* things to happen, as in the ubiquitous "inspired by" expression. Inspiration doesn't bring out your everyday engagement, it causes one to be *most engaged*. Psychologists call this "flow," "…a state of concentration so focused that it amounts to absolute absorption in an activity. Everyone experiences flow from time to time and recognizes its characteristics: people typically feel strong, alert, in effortless control, unselfconscious, and at the peak of their abilities" (Csikszentmihalyi, 1991, p. 1). Think of the many accomplishments that exist because of inspiration. While the concept of inspiration is universally familiar, it's hard to agree on one common definition. Inspiration can mean different things to different people. When artists and innovators are asked for their source of inspiration, they describe conditions: certain surroundings or circumstances, specific acts like routines, doodling, improvisation, going for walk, and other activities (Stenham et al., 2012). Companies can likewise set the stage for inspiration in a way that not only engages employees, but also encourages them to innovate. DOWE seeks to create environments where inspiration is uniquely defined and designed for flow.

Many of us would like to live our lives according to these principles — not just at work, but in everything we do. Unfortunately, many businesses are not run with purpose, mindfulness, meaning, and inspiration top of mind. Perhaps they don't know how and are waiting for something to show them. The choice to begin, however, is always present. People and organizations can work together to define these for themselves and make them a reality.

APPROACH

To begin DOWE, there are two prerequisites. First, you need to have a specific business reason for it, such as achieving organizational success or performance — something defined by your strategy and goals that can only be accomplished through people. Second, leadership must commit to playing a major role. As mentioned earlier, DOWE is neither a top-down nor a bottom-up approach. It is both: leadership (as representatives of the business) must be equally engaged *with* people (the employees) and vice-versa.

DOWE frames the workplace as a collection of smaller, interwoven experiences that make up an overall experience. Why? Because experience is how life is *lived* and *remembered*. Vijay Kumar of Illinois Institute of Technology defines it as the "act of living through events" (Kumar, 2013, p. 3). Disparate elements combine into something meaningful and memorable in experiences. Everyone has them, and understanding how others live through them builds empathy. They are what connects people – to each other, to a certain time, place, or happening. An actor described what the theater meant to him: "...you enter as an individual and you leave as a group because you've all been bound together by the same experience" (The Nerd Machine, 2013).

Marketers have long known this: "framing consumption as an experience rather than a single purchase decision is seen as a way for brands to provide greater value and forge deeper connections with consumers" (as said by Bhattacharjee & Mogilner, citing Pine & Gilmore, 1999 & Schmitt, 1999, p. 13). Work isn't lived as a series of transactions, but rather an amalgamation of memorable experiences, where DOWE seeks deeper, more positive connections. Structuring experiences as the basis of work life is also reminiscent of philosophy's phenomenology, the "study of everything we feel in the world, everything that gives our lives meaning...[shows us]...the essence of our relationship" to the things around us (Madsbjerg & Rasmussen, 2014, pp. 78–79). What is perceived by the senses is then interpreted into perceptions of experience. Because they happen in an ever-changing network of people and infrastructure, happenings in one place have the potential to impact other places. Indeed, a hallmark of design thinking is the holistic view known as systems thinking (Brown, 2009, p. 199). Seeing how the pieces affect each other and fit into the whole helps us to dig deeper into the organization's "underlying structures...made up of beliefs and assumptions, established practices, skills and capabilities, networks of relationships, and awareness and sensibilities ..." that are sometimes hidden despite their obvious influence (Senge, 2006, p. 286).

As mentioned before, DOWE also operates under the assumption that an organization's own people are qualified to study, affect, and create their own environment. This is derived from psychology's *Personal Construct Theory*, where what is predictable can be constructed – not to have identical experiences, but rather the *consistent interpretations* of an experience (Bannister, 1962, p. 108). This is what's referred to in DOWE as "setting the conditions." Those who can think like others within the same framework of experiences – i.e. *empathize* – can participate and even design on their behalf (Bannister, 1962, pp. 109–110), as members of the DOWE team do. This again speaks to the importance of and commitment to DOWE's *People & Context* as the starting point from which new and relevant experiences, strategies, and solutions can be designed.

There are two main players, the organization and its people, so DOWE solutions are both organization- and people-centered. Employees give and receive to the organizational experiences through their interactions. Their degree of engagement and their use of capabilities determine performance. For their part, organizations create the workplace itself and set the conditions in which those interactions occur. How these elements combine or interact are one-of-a-kind experiences and therefore require one-of-a-kind solutions. "In the same way participatory design seeks to 'ensure a better fit' between technology and the ways people (want to) perform work" (Kensing & Blomberg, 1998, p. 168), DOWE aims to do the same between an organization and its people.

One can appreciate the complexity of organizational life and the need for some way to make sense of it all. DOWE, with its use of empathy, insights, and connections, is the appropriate method to make sense of organizational life and to create new experiences purposefully and mindfully. The process reveals how the organization works today and what might work tomorrow. It demonstrates how to create outstanding experiences and transition the organization toward them. For this to take place, however, employees must be engaged to learn and grow in tandem with the organization. Hence, the DOWE process is structured to achieve all this through managing the interplay of DESIGN, CHANGE, CAPABILITY, and ENGAGEMENT.

METHODOLOGY

Every aspect of DOWE exists by design and with purpose, none of which are superfluous. To start, a designated team is charged with leading the work. There are arguments for why the "separate" piece is so important. In participatory design, "greenhouse settings" protect experimentation with new approaches outside the dysfunctions of the current state (Kensing & Blomberg, 1998, p. 175). Over 70 years ago, psychologist Kurt Lewin identified "cultural islands" where resistance is minimized and the potential for change is increased (Lewin, 1947, p. 37). Clayton Christensen, author of *The Innovator's Dilemma*, supports the belief that desirable disruption (such as new business models) can be successfully achieved "beneath a corporation's umbrella" as long as it is "set up separately" (Christensen, 2014, p. 44). These environments are not unlike the incubator settings of early start-ups, think tanks, or new business development within established companies. Barriers to co-creation in DOWE include the very culture that needs to change, unproductive cultural norms such as resistance, discouragement of collaboration in the name of privacy, territorial tendencies and turf wars, and the "not invented here" syndrome. Insulating the DOWE team from the restraints of the current culture gives freedom to create and model new working norms, even as a counterculture (if needed) (Lewin, 1947, p. 37). Indeed, the very practice of design thinking required by DOWE "cannot be seen separately from developing a culture conducive to design thinking (Prud'homme van Reine, 2017, p. 72)." In other words, practicing design thinking is a culture change in itself because it practices a new or different way of working. It brings its own dynamics. From their home base, the DOWE-Rs reach out to rest of the organization to validate designs and plans to ensure they "survive in 'real-world' settings" (Kensing & Blomberg, 1998, p. 175), as long as change is managed appropriately.

Preparations for DOWE set the design team up for success. Derived from extensive experience and research, these include role expectations and responsibilities, careful selection of team members, establishment of sufficient resources, physical and mental space to work, articulation of purpose and scope, early engagement and commitment of people, alignment, behavioral norms, and proper kickoff, launch and sunset. Here, the conditions for success are established *preemptively* instead of correctively. (Chapter 4 will explore these in greater detail.)

Once a team is in place, the DOWE process can begin (Figure 3.2). DESIGN comes from design methodology, which typically includes context (in-depth understanding of the current state), reframe (exploring possibilities and insights with different lenses), options (creation of new or different solutions or designs), and choose (disciplined selection of the best options). CHANGE incorporates actions known to support successful transformations.

Figure 3.2. DOWE Process (Detailed View).

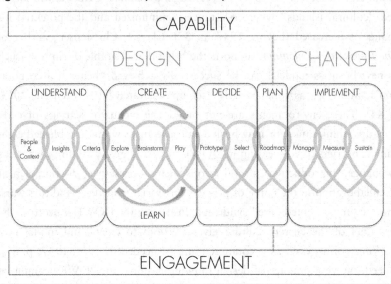

DESIGN and CHANGE breaks down into several phases, each with its own set of learning loops: *UNDERSTAND, CREATE & LEARN, DECIDE, PLAN,* and *IMPLEMENT.* These are also reminiscent of the steps in the Appreciative Inquiry (AI) 4-D model, which has a huge influence on DOWE: Discover, Dream, Design, Destiny (Cooperrider & Whitney, 2001). AI seeks to eradicate problems from leveraging the best of what works. This framing is profound. Problems are rendered obsolete if you create the circumstances where they can't exist. After all, they are symptoms of the greater context that pose a challenge – not challenge as in a disadvantage, but rather as a feat to achieve or overcome. Two beliefs in AI inspire the DOWE model most. The first is that "… human systems move in the direction of what they study" (Cantore & Cooperrider, 2013, citing Whitney et al., 2010, p. 272). The second comes from knowing that "… the social world in which we live is being continually co-constructed …" (Cantore & Cooperrider, 2013, p. 270). With these in mind, DOWE uses co-design (and thus co-creation in the process) to conscientiously research and explore toward a desirable future, together (Cantore & Cooperrider, 2013, p. 277). Having the benefits of co-design is advantageous to DOWE because it utilizes the perspectives, talents, and capabilities of an organization's people, engenders trust, and sets the stage for change adoption. Bottom line, people are more likely to embrace what they've helped create.

As a path to UNDERSTAND, DOWE uses learning loops to study *People & Context*, gain *Insights*, and establish *Criteria*. Activities are primarily driven by research and analysis techniques validated in organizational psychology, consumer research, cultural anthropology, and participatory design, such as data gathering methods, ethnographies, experiential interactions, and so on. Just like researchers in these fields, DOWE-Rs gain deeper knowledge from immersion with subjects in their native environments *without* unduly influencing the outcomes themselves. This takes "maintaining critical awareness of their own assumptions...checking and rechecking the ways their beliefs and actions might be shaping their research" as anthropologists do (Haviland, Prins, McBride, & Walrath, 2013, p. 5). Establishing norms, accountability, and maintenance of the DOWE team's own dynamics is needed on an ongoing basis to combat this and other potential pitfalls spanning the entirety of the initiative.

CREATE & LEARN covers what so many business "problem solvers" fail to exercise sufficiently before they converge on answers to complex questions. Decisions are deferred in favor of understanding the context in depth first and then giving new ideas proper development and exploration. Using co-creation and team collaboration, the DOWE process takes creating and learning, which are typically internal thinking mechanisms, and makes them external (Kolko, 2010). Once they are in the collective consciousness and have people's attention, phenomenology tells us that "the standpoint of idealism" then can be found "within itself" (Gadamer, 1982, p. 53). In other words, people can begin to truly envision the possibility of achieving the *best* solutions when they create through collaboration.

Through *Explore*, *Brainstorm*, and *Play*, viable options emerge through discovery rather than contrived from biased viewpoints. Ideas are examined exhaustively and mindfully, improving people's critical thinking, learning agility, and innovation skills at the same time. Groups of people may be brought in and out to contribute to *Play*, perhaps in small groups à la architecture charrettes or innovation-themed hackathons. Instead of making built environments or coding, they are molding concepts, creating experiences, and affecting culture. Various ideas are tinkered with in different settings, connected, taken apart, and recombined to become something new. What comes out might never exist if this part of the process is glossed over.

The delayed gratification rewards the organization with meticulously evaluated options. Rather than leading with preconceived notions, DOWE-Rs, in partnership with the organization's people, have iterated toward the solution(s) in a disciplined, yet creative manner.

DECIDE narrows the focus toward finding the best solutions. *Prototype* matures ideas with pilots and other activities that test reactions and scalability. All participants have a chance to be influencers. As DOWE enters *Select*, what remains is chosen based not on popular opinion, but on what best meets both business and employee criteria.

At least three cultural artifacts come out of the design process. The first is the Culture Study, a narrative created from comprehensive research of the organization's current state and its possibilities. The second is the Strategy and Design Blueprint, which captures the designed strategy, experiences and the ideas ultimately selected. The third is the Roadmap and Action Plans document, covering what and how the Blueprint will be implemented. As cultural anthropologists and organizational psychologists would attest, artifacts matter because they are a part of and considered reflections of aspirational and lived culture (Shockley, Thompson, & Andreassi, 2013, p. 311). Once these exist, they are a commentary on the organization's culture, reinforcing the building blocks for what's to come.

CHANGE demands as much discipline as DESIGN. It makes certain DOWE's output becomes part of the organization's way of work. This includes everything from launching the design all the way to its fully sustained integration. Much is known with regard to change management, though actual practice is often flawed. DOWE puts extra effort into change management *up front* to reduce chances of major remedial actions or catastrophe. PLAN creates the Roadmap and Action Plans for the Strategy and Design Blueprint to guide the forthcoming IMPLEMENT phase. Taking into consideration the way systems work, DOWE anticipates repercussions within the organization before, during, and after change at the individual, team, and organization levels. Actions are organized into engagement, learning, and communication categories — all key components of successful change efforts. Expertise from the marketing field (branding and messaging) and organizational psychology help DOWE structure and distribute information effectively, as intended. Planning accounts for all this, while also preparing the team to anticipate and deal with the unexpected.

IMPLEMENT sees to it that whatever is planned gets executed according to expectations (or better). By this point, change on a broad scale starts to feel like it's really happening, and progress can be observed in real time. *Manage*, *Measure*, and *Sustain* are needed to bring the organization toward the new experience with lasting impact.

This summary of the DOWE process is only a preview — Chapters 4–9 will explain everything in greater depth. Suffice it to say for now that all DOWE needs is people's talent and persistence to see it done.

DEBATING DOWE

It's fair game to consider DOWE as a devil's advocate, especially in the interest of advancing our understanding of how to improve workplace cultures and environments. DOWE is offered up as a different way to address serious gaps between where you are and where you want to be. If you look for them, you can find arguments for how DOWE might not work.

First, the process may be perceived as too unstructured for people's comfort. Once described and defined, it still leaves room for variability and incorporation of other outlooks, ideas, and methodologies. In other words, DOWE has the flexibility to stand on its own or to dovetail into other strategies of the organization. To illustrate: a company might use DOWE as the sole methodology to create or improve an employment experience that leverages diversity. Another company might decide to reorganize around a new business model and use DOWE to implement it successfully. DOWE provides a framework and philosophy that accommodates just about any type of work experience and business context, so it can't be too prescriptive without losing its versatility.

At the same time, DOWE encourages new methods, risk taking, and empowerment through CREATE & LEARN, and DECIDE. An organization's appetite for the process might determine whether DOWE is an appropriate cultural fit or intervention. People might express concern that these characteristics may only be acceptable in some national cultures and difficult to achieve in others. However, research indicates that strong corporate cultures are more salient (and therefore more influential) than national norms within the workplace if managed sufficiently (Pothukuchi, Damanpour, Choi, Chen, & Park, 2002). Most workers, regardless of nationality, ultimately want to do a good job in stimulating environments where they can contribute, learn, and develop. Enough leadership advocacy, employee engagement, and purposeful handling of the process from beginning to end will enable DOWE to do its good work, regardless of location.

Also, DOWE doesn't lend itself naturally to extensive empirical testing. If there's any concept that isn't suited for lab settings, it's this one. There is no attempt to control for variables, since they are considered part of the process. Contexts vary from organization to organization, greatly influencing how DOWE is used and carried out. That being said, DOWE is based on concepts proven in scholarship and in practice. The introduction of DOWE opens new research opportunities to explore *this particular combination* of proven methods and its outcomes. DOWE is also suited for meta-studies where scale is needed to net broad generalizations useful to everyone. Smaller comparisons simply have too much variability. Acknowledging that change takes time and institutional memory is lengthy, studying the effects of DOWE over a period of years would be beneficial to collective knowledge. Additional research will help DOWE evolve and perfect the stewardship of work cultures at the same time. Until then, DOWE's viability as a worthy organizational approach is a pass-fail exam. If used as intended and appropriately, it either works or it doesn't. When it works, it is exceptional. No matter the criticism, it's up to the individual organization to decide whether or not to choose DOWE. The choice is always there.

ROOM TO GROW

If you think about it, the DOWE process is an exercise in scientific integrity. It continually improves over a series of progressive learning loops that test hypotheses and theory in the field. It adds rigor and analysis to its conclusions without compromising scope or intent. Ironic that such discipline is required of DOWE when "people stuff" is often seen as a secondary priority to business and therefore managed inconsistently. Perhaps something like DOWE is what's needed to elevate the employee experience to the forefront of business.

So much of what makes up the DOWE concept and process is a tight web of multidisciplinary connections that are difficult to unravel. Still, there are many more connections to make, more insights to discover with every new DOWE initiative, and more experiences to be designed. What's known, through lived experience and research, is that DOWE works. It brings forth truly customized, impactful, successful people strategies and implementations for any number of limitless applications. Some of these will be explored in Chapter 10.

INTRODUCTION TO HOW-TO

With a conceptual understanding of DOWE, let's move on to explore what it looks like in action. The model itself is fairly straightforward. How it's done is the tricky part because DOWE-Rs must live up to its principles (purposeful, mindful, meaningful, and inspirational) and stay ahead of the dynamics within and around them. The unpredictability of human nature guarantees that designing and changing work experiences is complex and challenging. Conflicts and barriers to innovation, including those that originate with oneself, command attention. DOWE calls for the conscientious balance of opposing tensions—between boldness and fear, creativity and analysis, freedom and constraint, conservatism and risk, and so on.

One of the most common pitfalls throughout the DOWE process comes from pacing, i.e. the reconciliation of what's called satisficing and maximizing. This too is a balance. Coined by marketers to meld "satisfy" and "sacrifice," satisficing is the inclination to end efforts when only a minimum has been achieved. Doing so comes with risks, including falling short of the initiative's potential, failing to recognize and integrate pivotal information, or missing out on better options (Briley & Aacker, 2006, p. 60). DOWE-Rs must resist the temptation to thoughtlessly rush through steps in an attempt to move the process along or to meet an arbitrarily chosen deadline. This pitfall subtracts meaning and impact and makes you prone to mistakes. Maximizing, on the other hand, happens when the search for the best solution leads to never-ending overanalysis. This slows progress and mutes positive effects. The initiative inches along, coming to long-delayed decisions tainted by second guesses. The two extremes are equally detrimental and stem from a failure to understand how to pace the DOWE process. Equilibrium can be achieved when the team recognizes imbalance and works

47

together to identify the standards that must be met before moving on. This can happen at any point in the process and should be managed with care.

Particularly for first-time DOWE-Rs, the process will feel uncomfortable at times, even counterintuitive. The reality is that DOWE is actually pro-intuitive — it exercises sensemaking and connective thinking (hallmarks of intuition) to a great degree, perhaps more than what people are accustomed to. Discomfort sets in if DOWE operates in ways that are counter to the current culture or even an individual's personality. For example:

- Not every problem has only one solution

- Everything is framed in possibility, not absolutes (e.g., How might we...?)

- The path isn't direct or linear, left to right

- It is almost never what you think it is up front

- Failure is a way of learning

- Play is a good thing

All this being said, expect that members of the team may experience the occasional freak out at different points in the process. These occur in moments of weakness or during crises of faith, where one may be overwhelmed with fear or uncertainty. Also known as "moments of stark terror," they can come from self-doubt, in response to feedback, in the midst of drowning in data, after periods of intense activity, when decisions have to be made, or right before launch (Liedkta & Olgilvie, 2011, pp. 192–194). Being self-aware and in tune with others will surface these before they escalate. This is yet another advantage of working together as a team, where people can provide support and assurance in time of need. Be prepared to be there for each other, because everyone will need it at different times. When one person is feeling strong, another may have doubts, and vice versa. Help each other out.

Keep in mind also that if this is a new or different approach for the organization, all steps of the process may need multiple reviews, explanations, or attempts to satisfy DOWE's requirements. Be prepared to be patient and persistent throughout the learning process. Rest assured that the results eventually reveal themselves.

And finally, never forget that this work is intended to be an engaging development opportunity that sees the value in both success and failure.

Take this work seriously, but not too seriously — again, it's a balance. Somewhere in the journey, the uniqueness of the initiative will become evident, and through the transformation you will see how special it truly is.

As you read, remember that books present information sequentially. DOWE, however, is not linear, but progressive. You are invited to jump from section to section as the DOWE team focuses on various spaces within the model. Skip ahead if you want to know where this is going or go back to review something if you forget. Although information is provided here for big organizations tackling large-scale transformations, DOWE initiatives can vary in scope and size. Scale down as appropriate for your initiative, but make sure the DOWE team covers every learning loop. If you are testing DOWE out ahead of time, check out Chapter 10 on how to miniaturize or pilot DOWE.

This how-to section, Chapters 4–9, will guide the team step-by-step through the process, helping to maximize the potential of DOWE for meaningful impact. Building a stronger, richer, more productive culture is neither easy nor simple. DOWE provides the appropriate degree of structure to handle the complexity of organizational life. However, designing experiences calls for openness, commitment, persistence, and follow through on your part. Not only will you find the process doable, but also deeply rewarding. Let's begin.

CHAPTER 4

DOWE PREP

Topics covered in this chapter:

• Preparations for the DOWE initiative

• Expectations of the organization, its employees, and the DOWE team

• Establishment and selection of the DOWE team

• Setting the conditions for the team's success

> Important Reminder: DOWE is applicable for initiatives of any size, from small to large scale. The following chapters provide the how-to for the highest level of complexity, akin to enterprise-wide transformations in large companies. Everything here can be edited down or miniaturized, but make sure it is done without compromising the essence and intent behind DOWE.

Congratulations! You are about to embark on a great adventure with Design of Work Experience (DOWE). Change began from the moment you pondered new possibilities. Now it's up to you and your colleagues to make it a reality. The first step is to prepare your organization and its people.

Rarely are social contracts explicit, but the preparations for a DOWE initiative are presented here as such. Though literally signing this agreement isn't required, following these guidelines will ensure sufficient preparations are in place to set an initiative up for success. To make the most of DOWE, all participants are invited to read, discuss, and accept this agreement as a prerequisite and in preparation for the initiative.

DOWE EXPECTATIONS AND AGREEMENT

This is an agreement amongst the following:

1. Employees (also known as the users, people, and talent)

2. Core Design Team Members (also referred to as DOWE-Rs, team members, designers, researchers) who are collectively known as the core design team, DOWE team, research team, or self-named team of the DOWE initiative)

3. Organization (the company, business, non-profit, or agency as represented by leaders or executive sponsors)

Using DOWE, these groups will work together in partnership to innovate the selected experience (a.k.a. target, focus area, or subject), whether policy, process, interaction, organizational change, or any aspect related to perceived or experienced environment and culture.

Definitions

DOWE (pronounced ['dü 'wē]) partners employees with their employers to co-create customized and meaningful work experiences that set the conditions for people and business to thrive.

The DOWE process (also called the process, the model, the methodology) provides the structure and guidelines through which work experiences are created. These are represented as a collection of distinct activity spaces, which are arranged as progressive learning loops. Some actions come in and out intermittently, remain throughout the process, or require a number of iterations. The methodology ensures that whatever is designed becomes a reality through change, covering both the "what" and the equally important "how."

A DOWE initiative is a concerted organizational effort to follow the DOWE process in order to create and implement (1) a deep-dive Culture Study on the current state, including its strengths, complexities, and unmet needs; (2) a Strategy and Design Blueprint for the targeted experience (also referred to as the design, strategy, solutions, selected options or ideas, or design output); and (3) the Roadmap with associated Action Plans to implement the new experience.

Roles

In all DOWE initiatives, three parties of equal importance are involved, each with specific roles they must fulfill in order to be successful. Note that individuals may fall into more than one of these categories.

Employees: These are members of the community that represent the target group, the users of the organization for which the design is intended. They participate in user research and contribute to the design process as co-creators. They embody, live, and sustain the new experience. The success of the initiative is based upon the collective reactions of this group.

At least two subsets reside within the employees. First are the Early Adopters, a.k.a. EA'rs, connectors, change agents, and advocates. If designated, they lead, support, share, and evangelize on behalf of the DOWE initiative and the DOWE team. Managers, if they exist in the organizational structure, are expected to set expectations by example, provide support, coaching, and feedback, and to uphold commitment and accountability. This is in addition to their responsibilities as employees.

DOWE Team: The core design team members are curated from across the organization to design, manage, and roll out change from within. They interact with the users, lead the DOWE process on behalf of the organization, pilot the solutions, and ensure continuous improvement toward refined solutions that work. They also self-manage their own team dynamics throughout the initiative. The team functions collaboratively, without hierarchies, regardless of official titles or roles.

Executive Sponsors: As representatives of the business, these leaders support the initiative's success by setting direction and taking actions to lead and inspire people. As role models, they are expected to drive and sustain change by their attention, engagement, influence, and actions, inclusive of communications, active support, and encouragement. Sponsors provide physical and mental space for the core team and address and remove barriers as needed. This group expands as executive sponsors bring in more leaders during CHANGE.

Employee Responsibilities

Employees who participate through interactions with the DOWE team are volunteers who hold tremendous responsibility. They are positioned to affect their own workplace by co-creating for themselves and for others. Therefore, in addition to conduct and behaviors expected of all employees within the organization, they contribute as participants to the DOWE initiative as requested, including:

- Understanding that they are providing their own perspective. As a collective group, they speak for the whole, but no one individual speaks on behalf of others. Care should be taken to provide honest and authentic input in the spirit of enabling the organization to improve culture, environment, and experiences.

- Exercising their opportunity to contribute with their attention and engagement for DOWE activities.

- Providing feedback to the DOWE team to improve or address activities related to the initiative as necessary.

- Seeking to understand through collaboration and dialogue when questions arise, knowing that speculation or reticence can be subversive and destructive.

- Considering their role or congruity with the future state and direction of the organization, as all employees do every day.

- Taking ownership and action for their part in making the initiative successful. This includes holding oneself and others accountable to agreed upon expectations and enjoying the environment and experiences DOWE creates.

DOWE-R Responsibilities

No previous experience with design or DOWE is necessary. However, through this agreement and using the DOWE methodology, core team members commit to the following:

Mindset

- The DOWE-R understands and agrees that DOWE is learned by doing, experientially. Therefore, full appreciation for its usefulness and impact will only come through practicing DOWE over time.

- Team members adopt the described mindset and behaviors necessary to successfully practice DOWE. They trust the process and adhere to its general structure and intentions. It is the expectation to persist despite feeling unsure at times, especially during activities that are designed to be purposefully disruptive to the status quo.

- It should also be acknowledged that DOWE is not only a journey for the organization but also for the core design team. Doing DOWE is an "experience" in and of itself, an "experience within an experience." The team, as facilitators of DOWE, must manage their own experience responsibly. Members should initiate discussions and take preventative or remedial actions to preserve the optimum performance of the team as necessary.

- Team members see themselves not only as designers, innovators, learners, and researchers, but also as change agents who champion and model the collective vision going forward.

- The team will operate with no hierarchies. Regardless of background, level, or job titles, team members treat each other as respected peers, leverage each other's unique strengths and capabilities, and unite in delivering well-designed experiences.

- Once selected as a core design team, DOWE-Rs will be fully engaged. They seek to rectify any issues that could disengage themselves or other members of the team or organization.

Behaviors and Actions

- Dedication to the DOWE initiative is paramount. As with any successful team, all DOWE-Rs must be as equally and optimally invested as possible. Therefore, core team members must be engaged and physically and mentally present when needed. Scheduling and competing priorities should be a non-issue.

- Likewise, every member of the team participates in all phases of the DOWE process, even as people may take turns in leading different tasks and activities. This is not only crucial from a learning standpoint, but also supports a sense of shared ownership.

- As learners, DOWE-Rs have many opportunities not only to practice strengths, but also to try out new capabilities throughout the process. Team members commit to taking advantage of the chance to develop themselves in a safe learning environment.

- The DOWE team moves through the process at an appropriate pace that balances thorough exploration and reflection without overanalysis or fear-driven indecisiveness. The team defers judgment and conclusion until the appropriate time in the DOWE process. They take the position of true learners, remain open, and respect the journey toward achieving eventual conclusions. They will support and see through decisions once they are made.

- Additionally, members demonstrate behaviors described for each learning loop of the DOWE process.

- The team shall function as one cohesive body that leverages diversity of thought for greater returns. Bringing together different viewpoints does not mean members are there to represent any one point of view, group, or agenda, and there will be no competition for dominance. Rather, the diverse team serves as a reflection of the work community it seeks to affect, granting it at least some initial legitimacy with their users. Having the varied perspectives will also enrich deeper understanding of experiences and lead to better results. For an interdisciplinary team as design teams are intended to be, ownership and responsibilities are shared and/or mutually delegated.

- Every member of the DOWE team sees to it that the resulting design, along with associated strategies, roadmaps, and action plans, brings forth a tangible shift — that is, a marked, positive, difference between before and after. The team does so with the understanding that DOWE is not about re-creating the current state nor does it focus on what can't be done. It's attention remains on leveraging the strengths of the organization to enable new possibilities.

- Regardless of the target or focus area, the DOWE design team must model the vision of the future state or experience through their team-work. This is done knowing that the change in the organization begins with this team.

Organization Responsibilities

Executive sponsors, on behalf of the organization, promise the following:

- Leadership will establish vision and direction that aligns with and supports the achievement of business objectives and strategies. This includes taking great care to set the objectives without determining the answers. A description is written to describe the scope of the initiative (i.e. "target") and the corresponding type of DOWE team needed. This is done before any candidates are considered.

- The initiative may require budgetary support and access to resources. Leaders agree and understand that the size of the initiative and the impact of its activities are determined by resources made available. Sponsors will match the amount of resources to the appropriate scale to ensure success.

- Executive sponsors appoint a DOWE team to lead the organization through the process. By doing so, leadership will accept and support the design outcomes recommended by the team, with the knowledge that decisions are made with employee and business needs in mind.

- Leaders will engage and participate in DOWE, lending credibility for the initiative.

Selection of the Core Design Team

As with all talent management decisions, the business selects for the right persons in the right roles in the right environment. The business need is articulated and considered before pairing with suitable talent. Leading with specific individuals in mind risks departure from organizational need or intent. Therefore, prior to selection, executive sponsors will ensure candidates:

- come from within the target organization

- offer unique strength, capability, work style, experience, perspective, or expertise that doesn't exist on the team

- display well-roundedness and propensity for new ways of thinking and working

- are available to be dedicated

- are excited, willing, and interested in the project and prepared to persist through hard work to attain worthy goals

- are in good standing within the organization (i.e. not under disciplinary or performance improvement review)

Teams may also be formed under the following scenarios:

- Executive sponsors may originate or participate as members of the DOWE team but must take great care to work with the team as peers. Their role or level cannot influence the team any more than other individual members.

- An individual or two may instigate the DOWE initiative as a passion project as long as they meet candidate requirements. They work with their executive sponsors to craft what is needed for the team and select remaining members from there.

- If the organization has a preexisting culture team or committee, they (or a subset) can serve as possible candidates for the DOWE team, as long as they are vetted appropriately.

The size of the team will be determined by the organizational context. Generally, a smaller team may suffer a dearth of diverse experiences or perspectives, while a larger team can range from high cohesiveness to fractured team dynamics. A team should ideally target 4–8 members, selected in collaboration with organization leaders to support buy-in and diversity.

However, if an organization is small enough (20 or fewer, or individual teams or departments) the design team *is* everyone. A small core team may exist to manage the process and engage with everyone else as participants, but all in the organization are involved.

Setting the Conditions for Core Design Team Success

The executive sponsors understand that a team of experienced designers may only need the resources and space to do what they do best. In organizations where design is a new or developing capability for those involved, additional support for the team will be considered, such as:

- a team coach who knows DOWE, or at minimum, the design process. Whether this resource is internal or external to the organization, their primary purpose is to help the team navigate through the process. DOWE-R's must do all the designing.

- various experts to provide stimulus for the team in their target subject matter. These resources may step in and out based on need and do not do work intended for the team. They are resources for inspiration and stimulus only.

- additional people resources or technology for high-volume work, such as collecting, sorting, analyzing user research, or planning change implementation. This may come in the form of an internal team of ethnographers, an external firm who specializes in ethnography or from a cadre of Early Adopters (EA'rs). Need for these resources depends on the size of the initiative.

Executive Sponsors give the core design team at least three types of space:

- *physical working space* – This is a place that can be used as a "war room" or staging area. As the primary users, the space should be of the team's own design. This gives them the opportunity to model use of the workspace to connect people, encourage healthy interactions, and create an environment for continuous learning that fuels creativity and innovation.

- *virtual working space* – User research and other parts of the DOWE process yield a volume of information that needs organization, accessibility, and version control. Virtual shared folders, collaboration software, and other technology can facilitate their work.

- *adequate mental space* – This space is as important, if not more important, than all other spaces needed by the team. Executive sponsors resist the urge to micromanage or even hover and yet they must also consistently show interest and engagement. The DOWE team should be given the freedom and latitude to create and execute. Occasional steering or executive committee updates or working sessions can give the team and their sponsors opportunities to check in and align on direction. The operative word here is *occasional* because preparing for these meetings is disruptive to the train of thought and the process itself. If the team is not full-time on the project, work is prioritized to neutralize all other competing priorities to keep members focused when working on DOWE.

Initiative Kickoff

A formal kickoff heralds the beginning of the DOWE initiative and sets aside the time for the design team to focus on formation activities such as getting to know one another, building team self-awareness, and establishing operational norms. A multi-day off-site (~2−5 days) is recommended to form early team cohesion through a memorable, shared experience, with at least one overnight to cultivate the conditions, percolate ideas, and to reflect on learning. Having fun planning the kickoff is highly encouraged, and there are many ways to do it. In general, a proper kickoff should include:

- An overview of the DOWE concept, principles and process along with what to expect

- A grounding in the business need for the initiative

- Foundational knowledge of the topic/focus

- Work on self-awareness and how it contributes to team dynamics

- Contracting of team norms and operating principles

- Multiple opportunities for informal social interaction

- Planning of immediate next steps to begin work

Speakers are optional, though having a good facilitator or your DOWE coach is recommended. Having them lead the meetings allows the team to focus on being participants and on each other.

In addition to being a positive experience, the kickoff should produce:

- Revised description of the DOWE initiative's purpose, scope, anticipated challenges, and the expected outcomes to be aligned with executive sponsors and validated through user research.

- A plan for individual and team development opportunities on the DOWE team itself, with observable measurements identified.

- Team covenants/charters. These incorporate commitments that are established to set the tone for the working relationships as a team. They include norms, behaviors, and agreements on operating principles, governance, and how decisions are made. They end up creating a shared, living document to be referred to throughout the initiative, which may be amended or recontracted as necessary. It also informs others how the team works and demonstrates commitment to cultivating team dynamics and health regardless of workload or activity. As the team exists to innovate, norms and behaviors are adopted to foster innovation (*See Appendix A for the sample Team Charter Template*).

- The DOWE design team is encouraged to name themselves and discuss the desired perception they want to promote in their communications and interactions. Identity and affinity with the team is as important as cohesion because it nurtures adaptive learning and performance (Van Der Vegt & Bunderson, 2005, p. 535).

- Initial work plans. The core team needs structure to begin the work. Drafting initial plans for workspace and the *People & Context* activities call upon the team to organize, think holistically, and to identify immediate needs or gaps that haven't been acknowledged previously.

DOWE Team Dynamics

Once DOWE is in-flight, it is difficult to retroactively fit in time to focus on within-team dynamics. Touch points where the topic is discussed should be scheduled and adhered to on a regular basis (daily, weekly, biweekly, or by phase), depending on preference. Team scorecards may be adopted as a springboard for discussion (see Figure 5.6 as an example). In-depth comprehensive reviews (every 3–6 weeks or monthly) explore actual team dynamics in comparison to commitments and norms, celebrate and leverage strengths and successes, and resolve possible conflicts or dysfunctional patterns actively or preemptively. These activities support the balance that must be made between team cohesion and diversity of thought. In addition:

- Members of the team demonstrate their commitment by holding themselves and each other accountable to agreed-upon norms and development areas.

- Individuals of the team comprehend that they will also experience change along with the rest of the organization. This may include extreme states such as being overwhelmed or overly enthusiastic. Self-awareness can be maintained through reflection. Initiative is taken to call out and resolve issues such as outstanding conflicts, work fatigue, and other possible pitfalls.

- The team understands that adequate cultivation of team dynamics will leverage diversity and encourage healthy debate and robust discussions.

- Efforts will be made to maintain team cohesion where members proudly identify and value participation on the team.

Milestones and Sunset

Milestones throughout the DOWE process are opportunities to track and recognize progress. The DOWE team collaborates with the business to discuss how this should be managed and shared. Completion of DOWE learning loops or phases can also be considered as achievements. The PLAN phase will establish key milestones throughout implementation.

The DOWE design team and the business also determine the best time to sunset the initiative some time after *Sustain* activities are in place. Measures are taken to maintain sustainability and continuity after the conclusion of major activities. Equal care and attention should be made for the DOWE finale as there is for kickoff. Activities include:

- Knowledge transfer and transition planning to ongoing owner(s) of the initiative's outcomes

- Recognition

- Reflective learning and after-action review

- Final versions of documentation, including the Culture Study, Strategy and Design Blueprint, Roadmap and Action Plans

- Discussion and planning of what happens next

Acceptance

Upon acceptance, all participants will promise to carry forth the responsibilities and actions outlined in this agreement.

Name:

Initiative:

The initiative commences upon acceptance of this agreement and mutually agreed upon timelines.

Agreed By on DATE

_____

Names and Signatures of DOWE Team and sponsors

CHAPTER 5

UNDERSTAND

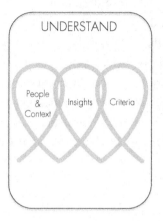

UNDERSTAND OVERVIEW

The power of DOWE hinges upon experiences, solutions, and strategies created from a deep understanding of the current context. It begins with seeking first to UNDERSTAND and resisting the urge to go straight from problem to solution. Organizational self-awareness goes beyond what you "think" you know about the culture to knowing and understanding its hidden complexities. The DOWE team uncovers the organization's underlying circumstances (a.k.a. conditions), goes behind what people say to what they actually do, articulates the unmet needs of the organization, builds insights and criteria that will inform the development of solutions, and describes a comprehensive picture of the organization and its people. Self-awareness is so important because it uncovers the needs, motivations, strengths, development opportunities, and the rationale behind people's behaviors and sheds light on how to manage oneself and others. To know thyself paves the way to improve thyself. The DOWE team facilitates the building of organizational self-awareness in UNDERSTAND, cultivates their own self-awareness as individuals on a team, and helps others to become more self-aware. Through the course of this, they leverage and develop CAPABILITY.

The Culture Study, a narrative document and accompanying multimedia (visuals, sound bites, and others), is the product of UNDERSTAND. It is a summary and analysis that calls out the explicit and the implicit – that is, the obvious and the not-so-obvious aspects of the culture that have significant impact on the work experience. It documents the team's journey and provides a reference for future people initiatives. This organizational self-awareness paves the path toward genuine change.

For a sample Table of Contents from a Culture Study, see the Appendix B.

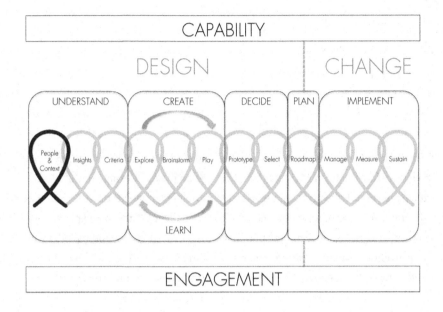

PEOPLE & CONTEXT

<u>Input:</u> Team's Perspective and User Research

<u>Output:</u> Culture Study

<u>Mindset:</u>

- Be open, impartial, thoughtful, analytical, and positive

- Stay curious

- Be intuitive

- Remain people and other-centered

<u>Behaviors:</u>

- Assume different perspectives

- Pay attention, observe

- Show empathy

- Practice creativity

- Engage and connect with others

- Follow through

- Learn

Aligning Purpose and Scope

The bulk of *People & Context* is devoted to research and analysis, but the work begins before the team interacts with their first employee. Coming out of kickoff, the team should already have the first step in building context: the description of the initiative's purpose, scope, its anticipated challenges, and the expected outcomes. This aligns the team, the initiative's executive sponsors, and the organization around a common starting point. Now aim to state a clear and finite purpose with impact. Identify only what is most important, in scope, and why.

Challenge yourselves to write the purpose and scope in one pithy phrase or sentence.

With this constraint, the team will have to think through what they are really trying to do. The purpose should include a clear, direct link to the business goals and strategies driving the DOWE initiative. What's the ambition level for the organization? Is it looking to improve upon the known, expand the boundaries, or change the game (Keeley et al., 2013, pp. 136–137)? Framed in such a way, the statement signals that DOWE is not another feel good pet project or fad, but rather a means to tangible, impactful change.

Once the statement is drafted, test it. Challenge the statement by asking and answering "Why?" five times (Collins & Porras, 1996, p. 70). This adds discipline to the thought process and gets to the *real* purpose. Begin with the objective identified by the executive sponsors, for example:

> *This [describe DOWE initiative] does X [ambition] for [this reason].*
>
> *Why?* (Because they said/think so)
>
> *Why?* (Because of a perceived [specific] business or people problem)

Why? (The possible [specific] opportunity)

Why? (The benefit(s) of the opportunity)

Why? (The real reason to desire those benefit(s))

The statement should delineate the boundaries within which the DOWE team can freely move, and it becomes the standard by which any related projects must align.

Identifying Early Assumptions and Key Questions

At this time, DOWE-Rs also present their own view of the current state and identify their assumptions as a separate section in the narrative. The team predicts what they expect to see. *From the DOWE perspective, predictions are the same as biases.* Exposing predictions compels the team to confront and address their assumptions up front and let go of them as necessary. It allows user research to prove, disprove, or assert something new altogether. There is always the proclivity for bias to influence perspectives, and exposing predictions helps to safeguard against this.

Key questions are then raised not only for the upcoming user research but also for shaping the initiative as a whole. Oftentimes these are paradoxes the organization has been unable to adequately address in the past, major challenges that must be overcome, or identified key opportunities. For example:

- "Our workplace is known for work–life balance, flexibility, and autonomy. Why is it that employees are still unsatisfied?"

- "Why have previous diversity initiatives failed despite stakeholder demands?"

- "How can we manage a major transformation without disrupting business continuity?"

- "We lack a talent management strategy that enables us to innovate. How do we develop one that works when we have failed before?"

Remember to include Early Assumptions and Key Questions in the Culture Study narrative prior to user research as a documentation of the journey.

User Research Preview

People & Context requires a willingness on the part of the organization to be open to genuine self-examination that reveals both the good and the bad. This degree of honesty and depth of understanding is a necessary ingredient for building authentic solutions later on. Recall from Chapter 1 that context includes business factors, culture, environment, behaviors, and experiences. Gather all the relevant materials necessary to understand business factors: strategies, reports, presentations, conversations with leadership, and so on. These are inputs for *People & Context* to be incorporated.

The people aspects of the context (culture, environment, behaviors, and experiences) are captured through user research — or if you'd prefer — employee research. User research is like consumer research, but the focus is on employees rather than shoppers or end users. The objective is to get to know employee experiences, perceptions, and behaviors through various angles. To do this, the team must see their role at this stage of the process as seeking out and articulating the voice of the employees — not their own. Here, they are researchers, looking to gain knowledge that leads to new understanding. Truly representing the voice of the employee requires skills in observation, active listening, reflection, and empathy. The opportunities to use these skills should be evident in the selection of multiple methodologies that capture the organization from different points of view, including individual, team, and organizational levels, as well as short-term, mid-term, and long-term experiences. To the best of their abilities, the researchers use inquiry and observation to *explain, not judge or excuse,* the true current state.

Mindset influences how DOWE-Rs interact with users and should therefore be conscientiously managed. Remember, "it's not about 'us versus them' or even 'us on behalf of them.'" For the design thinker, it has to be 'us *with* them,'" in thought and approach (Brown, 2009, p. 58). User research thus serves a dual purpose. In addition to providing rich information on the organization's culture and experiences, the research interactions engage employees and provide an opportunity for them to collaborate on and commit to the future.

How employees feel coming out of their participation will influence whether they support the work, how they behave, and what they tell people when they go back to their daily work life. These could be the same people who will eventually champion the design they inspired. Even at this early stage, take advantage of user research as an opportunity to create buy-in for DOWE and its eventual results, while also increasing engagement through connective, meaningful interactions.

The bottom line for *People & Context* is this: *the direction and effectiveness of the initiative depends on the depth and quality of employee research.*

Planning User Research

User perspective can be gathered in countless ways, and the dashboard of methodologies is as unique as your initiative and your organization. This book will not prescribe which methods to use because they are selected based on context and topic.

For illustrative purposes, however, data collection techniques can include:

• ethnographies

• interviews

• real or simulated work activities or meetings

• small group exercises

• daily diaries

• office visits

• video or photo blogs

• experience maps or drawings

Methods can come from or be inspired by tools already existing in design, human factors, and anthropological, psychological, consumer, and marketing research. Vijay Kumar's *101 Design Methods* and *The Designing for Growth Field Book* by Jeanne Liedtka, Tim Ogilvie, and Rachel Brozenske are treasure troves of possibilities and starting points.

The DOWE team might also create or modify their own methods, as long as they can observe, capture data, or interact with users. Each technique should elicit honest information about the current context – good, bad, or indifferent, significant or seemingly insignificant (but possibly important). Encourage unsolicited stories or descriptions of firsthand experiences in bulk, for they are evidence or analogies of greater truths (Garvin, 2000, p. 64).

Here are some pointers on how to select the right combination:

- *Use multiple methods*: Any social scientist will attest that every methodology by itself has its limitations. Using a variety of methods, both qualitative and quantitative, offsets some of these limitations and provides perspective from different vantage points. Experience shows that having three to five methods is optimal; more than five extends the time it takes to complete research and can be redundant.

- *Cast the net wide*: Don't just settle for previously used methodologies. Surveys, questionnaires, and focus groups are the common go-to methods for many organizations. Consider limiting their use due to familiarity, propensity for leading questions, and self-reported (and therefore possibly flawed) data.

  Multiple choice questions are especially limiting. By their design, they are narrowly framed, leading users to respond exclusively to the questions given. Independent thinking is never teased out. Instead, reverse it: conduct research first and then assign multiple choices as common answers or themes. If you do choose to use questionnaires, get a basic understanding of the topic and use resources such as the Survey Quality Predictor online to improve the quality of your survey design.

  Traditional focus groups (i.e. Tell me how you feel about specific X) don't lend themselves to profound insights. The vocal few speak while others listen. People often refuse to disagree or lend differing opinions in a group setting. If focus groups are chosen as one methodology, keep them small (<10) to encourage everyone's participation.

  Introducing new types of interactions signal to everyone else that DOWE is going to be different. As a result, it compels them to be more thoughtful in their responses. Be open and seek out a variety of tools, even new ones.

- *Assess Effectiveness*: Use methods that actually get people to respond and provide accurate data. The intent is to challenge the status quo, but not to the degree where participants reject the activity out of discomfort or unfamiliarity. If one method results in low participation or interest, then explore the root causes of that apathy or disengagement and choose another backup method. Creating a safe environment where people can be earnest and authentic is critical. Watch out for participant fatigue, where the task of providing feedback may be too frequent and/or labor intensive. Half-baked or lazy responses lead to bad data.

- *Offer Variety*: Research methods should permit different levels of time commitment to be distributed across the user base – some participants might be engaged once and only briefly, others might participate in multiple interactions by choice, and still others may volunteer for deep dive explorations that could add up to several hours over a period of weeks. Give people choices for the degree they want to donate their time or involvement.

- *Behavior-based Activities*: Self-reporting methods can be limiting, so seek methods where the core team can observe behaviors firsthand, like those in activity-focused research. Remember it's not just what is said but also what people do – these are not always the same. Thomas Edison understood this distinction. He was known to forego interviews in favor of having candidates work with his teams for a period of time. If they added value and worked well with them, then they got the job offer. In real-life scenarios such as this, it is very difficult for someone to fake their way through it.

- *Get Out*: The team should conduct research out in the field, in people's immediate work areas, where possible. Gathering information where day-to-day experiences and interactions take place can help to limit the impact of the researcher's presence on the environment or the results.

- *Make it Fun*: Participation should be voluntary (people want to partake, not because they have to), so activities need to be stimulating and engaging. If it's boring, engagement goes down.

For accurate results, it's essential that participants feel safe to provide information without fear of reprisal – be prepared to offer reassurances to reinforce this as needed. Again, at this point in the process, it is absolutely paramount that the data gathered come from *users* themselves, untainted by the design team.

Whatever the methodology, every question must be broadly framed to avoid leading the users. Follow-up or probing questions should also remain broad, such as "Tell me more." "Help me understand." "What does that mean and why?" Steer clear of setting expectations, other than to say,

"There are no right or wrong answers. Your honest perspective is the right answer." Body language and reactions must also be consciously managed to convey friendly neutrality on the part of the researchers.

Selecting Users

Once methods are selected, the next step is to organize the users. In a larger organization, a cross section of employees is all that's needed to capture major vantage points or group demographics. A nonscientific but experience-proven guideline might start at 10% of the target organization. In smaller settings, the team can afford to engage everyone in different ways.

Be mindful and purposeful about framing and communicating the initiative when recruiting volunteers. Provide a basic understanding of the work, why it's needed, what it hopes to achieve, and the compelling reasons to get involved. Be aware, however, that despite best efforts, misperception can still arise. For example, one DOWE initiative, despite its intent to develop talent, was rumored to be a secret project to fire people. As long as misunderstandings don't adversely impact the initiative as a whole, the DOWE design team can disprove rumors through their own behavior, communications, and their interactions. If misperceptions cause disruption, the DOWE team or their executive sponsors may need to intervene, especially when neglecting to do so may prove harmful in the long run.

No matter where the data comes from, the DOWE design team must allow the content stand on its own, *considering only what was said and not who said it*. Demographic cuts can lend some perspective to the raw data, but the reputation or personality of the individual user shouldn't be a factor. All participants should be treated as equally important and relevant. Assign numbers to users or decouple the data from the user altogether to minimize bias and guarantee anonymity. A contract or confidentiality agreement between users and the design team might seem like overkill in some contexts, but reassuring and respectful in others. Decide how to handle this.

Sort the list of users and match their availability to time required. Then randomly assign them to the methodologies within each time category (Figure 5.1).

The process can become too political or contrived if people get to choose their interaction or if the team chooses for them. There is less reason to get

Figure 5.1. Matching Users to Methodology.

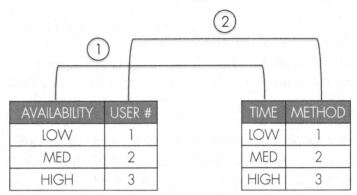

upset if it is up to chance to decide, as long as the team sticks with randomization.

Don't forget new hires. They offer a unique perspective that can be helpful to research. Coming from a different work environment, they can observe their new employer with fresh eyes. Comparing their perspectives with those who have been in the culture for a longer period of time can lead to unexpected and useful insights.

If applicable to your context, former employees of the organization can provide another vantage point, as long as they left on good terms. If they're open to a discussion, they can explain their reasons for leaving and offer comparisons, ideas, and advice. The alumni experience, as in life after leaving the company, may also be worthy of further exploration as a design opportunity.

Interacting with Users

Finally, the interactions can begin. As said before, this must be a positive experience for participants. For live sessions, researchers should:

- Conduct themselves as learners.

- Create a safe environment, reinforcing trust, and confidentiality.

- Permit the user to contribute without suggesting answers.

- Give the user ample time to think. Pauses or moments of silence in conversation may be needed to let them process their thoughts.

- Practice active listening to ensure information is accurately captured and understood. When in doubt, check for understanding.

- Remain flexible and diverge from protocol if appropriate. Facilitation should balance completing the exercise without shutting down vital input from users. Serendipity has been known to originate some key insights. There's always an option to schedule a part II in order to finish if needed.

- Show gratitude for their participation and contribution.

One advantage of having a DOWE team is the ability to share workload. For the sake of learning, every team member participates in all phases of the process. However, not everyone needs to interact with every user on every methodology. Splitting up responsibilities and then coming back together to discuss findings is highly encouraged and part of how the DOWE process works from a practical standpoint.

Research yields a tremendous amount of data. It is up to the DOWE team to decide how this material is stored, organized, and accessed. One team purchased foam core boards that stood roughly eight feet high, creating "walls" that were easily movable. Then they cut and pasted pieces of the user data on the boards, pinned up relevant articles, and used sticky notes to denote groupings by theme. Another group simply used the walls available to them while working and then preserved their sorting with plastic bags (see Figures 5.2 and 5.3). Teams can

Figure 5.2. Sorting Data.

Figure 5.3. Data Storage.

discover their best way for keeping track of data through trial and error, whether it is with boards, mind maps, graphs, databases, spreadsheets, etc. The system need not be hi-fidelity, just effective. Regardless, data needs to be organized to facilitate the next step, the discovery of insights.

Self-Understanding

Understanding *People & Context* includes individual members of the core design team. To reinforce the principles of DOWE (mindful, purposeful, meaningful, and inspirational), set aside time for reflection as part of the scheduled team check-ins/touchpoints established during kickoff. Reflection supports meaning-making as each person interprets and reinterprets what goes on (Marsick, Sauquet, & Yorks, 2006). People automatically do this, though not always consciously. If necessary, systematic training in mindfulness can make the endeavor more purposeful and overt (anonymous, personal communication, January 14, 2015).

Start with individual reflection that focuses on solidifying lessons learned and building self-awareness. Review and ponder the significance of new knowledge, what's going on, how things are going, how each team member is doing, what makes sense or not, what feels right or not. Then go deeper and consider motivations, conditions, and root causes for what works and doesn't work.

Ask critically reflective questions: What else is going on? What hasn't been considered but has an impact on the situation? How has the past informed perspective? Is the framing accurate? Are there other ways to interpret things (Marsick et al., 2006, p. 494)? Visualize the topic at the center of a circle and consider different perspectives or explanations surrounding it. Think through which patterns in the team's dynamic should be replicated and which should be broken. Build awareness of personal agendas because it affects judgment and behavior (Beal & Weiss, 2013, p. 18). Keep a journal or take notes. Come up with ideas or plans for action.

Then come together as a group. Some DOWE teams develop their own "barometers," an example is represented in Figure 5.4. This is one way to gauge individual perspective (in this case, energy level), and see how it translates to the whole of the team. This also serves as a conversation starter to address what increases or decreases energy on the team (Figure 5.4).

Another tool used in reflection is Marsick and Watkins's Informal and Incidental Learning Model (Figure 5.5). Arranged like the cardinal points

Figure 5.4. Team Barometer.

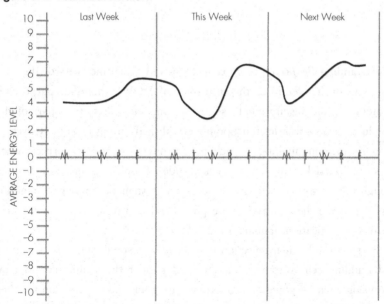

Figure 5.5. Marsick and Watkins' Informal and Incidental Learning Model.

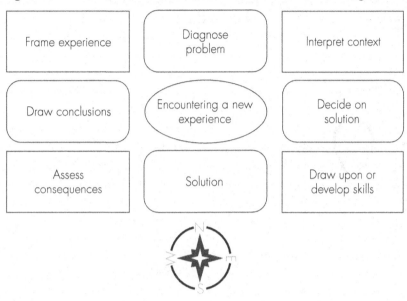

(North, South, East, West), the model starts at the north and goes clockwise around encounters. Though this particular model highlights problems and solutions, be sure to include opportunities and advantages as well.

With or without a tool, reflect and discuss what's going on as a group in a nonjudgmental way. A downside of reflection is that it happens after the fact. However, if done on a regular basis, this limitation can be offset with smaller, real-time adjustments. Members of the team can support each other and be inspired to come up with new ideas as a result.

Discuss how the individual reflections (such as learning, conclusions, perceptions or ongoing themes) play off each other through team dynamics. Give and get feedback. Call out patterns of dysfunction and resolve them. Revalidate or revise team charters, covenants, and norms. Agree on actions to perform better as a team. Resist the temptation to repeat mistakes by skipping over things that could make a critical difference in the outcome of the initiative. All this enables the team to practice DOWE on behalf of the organization and its people.

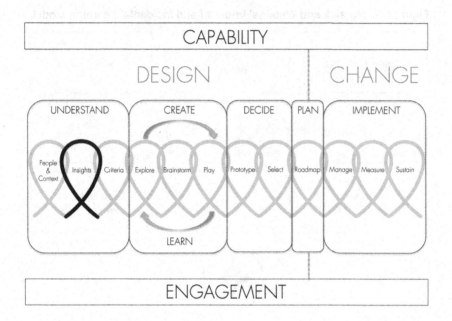

INSIGHTS

<u>Input:</u> User Research

<u>Output:</u> Culture Study (insights, validation, provocative proposition, visuals)

<u>Mindset:</u>

- Think connectively

- Be open, reflective, and intuitive

- Stay curious

<u>Behaviors:</u>

- Ask questions

- Engage and collaborate

- Organize your thinking

- Check understanding with others

- Learn

- Demonstrate empathy – honor the employee POV

Materials related to user research and Business Factors (as described in Chapter 1) yield a treasure trove of raw data, perhaps to an overwhelming degree. The employees have entrusted the core design team to incorporate all this input and feedback. Now the DOWE team must work to synthesize the data into patterns and then meaningful insights that communicate a deep understanding of the context. From there, the team validates or invalidates predictions and assumptions, articulates the future vision in the form of a provocative proposition, and visually summarizes the current context. All these contribute to the narrative of the Culture Study.

Insights Defined

Insight [in-sahyt] n.

1. An instance of apprehending the true nature of a thing, especially through intuitive understanding.

2. Penetrating mental vision or discernment; faculty of seeing inner character or underlying truth.

Source: dictionary.com

An "insight" is a remarkable realization that you could leverage to better respond to a design challenge. Insights often grow from contradictions between two user attributes or from asking yourself "Why?" when you notice strange behavior.

Source: https://dschool-old.stanford.edu/groups/ k12/wiki/97f30/…/c6f3c/empathytools.pptx

On the surface, insights are the pithy statements based on analysis of the raw data, but the experience of insight building is so much more than that. As a necessary part of the DOWE process and a powerful tool, insights give the core design team the ability to outwardly connect and integrate each member's internal thought processes, while also managing the tension between narrow and broad perspectives. Insights reflect what the design team thinks is going on in the context. It speaks to the "inner nature" or the essence of what the DOWE-Rs have observed (Kumar, 2013, p. 139).

High-quality insights:

- are written in the voice of the employee ("I...", "We....")

- are an inference; not always obvious

- represent what is being said by employees directly *and* indirectly

- are supported by and only reflect what's said by the employees (with no projections from the DOWE team)

- answer:
  - What is the data saying about the big picture?

  - What does it mean?

  - What is occurring? Why?

  - What's the impact?

- provide deeper, more profound understanding of the employee experience

- delineate which aspects of the experience are shared and what varies from person to person

- pull out what appear to influence the work experience and people's behaviors within them

Insights and insight building comes down to DOWE-Rs' use of curiosity, inquiry, and empathy to collaboratively interpret the employee viewpoint, in profound ways that inform the innovation process. After thorough, thoughtful examination and deliberation of the current context, they use insights to describe what they learned from the research and what the team understands about the user experience. They are the interpretation of what the *collective voice of the user* is saying – as a whole group, not individually. Insights can't be created formulaically – that is, you don't do a, b, c to get x, y, z. Through the process of seeking and interpreting patterns, DOWE-Rs gain clarity about people and their experiences. Like an Easter egg hunt, the team has to look everywhere in order to find their prizes. Patterns are discovered only when the team lets go of their own preconceived notions and becomes intimate with the data – all of it – to the degree that it's internalized and understood as second nature.

Keeping a user-centered perspective means all interpretations of the world happen exclusively through the eyes of the employees. Therefore, all insights must originate and trace back to *a set* of raw data. It's important for DOWE-Rs to maintain the role of the researcher, making sure that empathy does not turn into bias for any subset of the user base. They must also avoid the tendency to project their own opinions onto the data. One such team contended with this when a member, sensitive to what makes people "feel bad," interpreted raw data using that filter. This was due in part to this person's own experiences of "feeling bad" at work themselves, in ways that really influenced how they viewed the company. Other DOWE-Rs gently probed to uncover this personal bias, negotiated with the perspective, and emerged with a balanced view as a team. When a team develops insights, members must hold each other accountable to avoid these and other pitfalls. Challenge each other to find patterns in the data as evidence and support for the interpretations.

In this age of machine learning, artificial intelligence, and innovation in the data sciences, it may be tempting to use technology to shortcut this part of the process. However, there is not yet a viable replacement for the brilliance of the human mind, and nothing to replace our ability to use intuition and empathy. The DOWE team must be able interpret the human experience from a place of deep understanding, and that requires intimacy with the data that only comes from working with it.

The Insight Building Mindset

Learn by doing. This is especially true when it comes to the development of insights. As one DOWE-R put it, "I don't think that any amount of preparation ahead of time would have made a difference. We couldn't know how deep it was going to go until we got there" (anonymous, personal communication, January 9, 2015). Until then, these pages are a description of what can only be appreciated in the act itself, similar to explaining a new color without actually seeing it. Overthinking and becoming paralyzed by the data or jumping to conclusions too quickly without proper reflection are all possible risks to be avoided. Working in collaboration with others will calibrate this balance through experimentation and shared learning.

Understand that this activity isn't about completing *the task* of developing insights. Going through the motions wastes time and nets insights that either won't mean anything or are inaccurate. It is, first and foremost, about sensemaking and learning. This way of thinking is what makes insight building a valuable tool.

As intangible and elusive as insights may be, there are tools that can help designers to activate them. Assume a "beginner's mindset" or as IDEO partner and author Tom Kelley would call it, "thinking like a traveller." Look at things as one would for the first time in a new place. This gives "the ability to 'see' what's always been there, but has gone unnoticed – what others have failed to see or comprehend because they stopped looking too soon" (Kelley, 2005, p. 18). Assuming a beginner's mindset and thinking like a traveller may be awkward and difficult at first, but everyone is equipped to do this.

How to Assume A Beginner's Mindset

Don't judge. Just observe and engage users without the influence of value judgments upon their actions, circumstances, decisions, or "issues."

Question everything. Even (and especially) the things you think you already understand. Ask questions to learn about how the user perceives the world. Think about a 5-year-old who asks "Why?" a hundred times.

Be truly curious. Strive to assume a posture of wonder and curiosity, especially in circumstances that seem either familiar or frightening.

Find patterns. Look for interesting threads and themes that emerge across interactions with users.

Listen. Really. Lose your agenda and let the scene soak into your psyche. Absorb what users say to you and how they say it, without thinking about the next thing you're going to say.

Source: https://dschool-old.stanford.edu/groups/k12/revisions/4e22d/2/ Creative Commons Attribution.

Figure 5.6. Sorting for Insights.

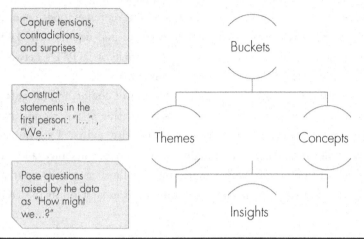

Developing Insights

Step 1. Gather all fragments, ideas, quotes, comments, multimedia, and other materials from user research and embark on a series of iterative sorting that determines the team's organization of the raw data (Figure 5.6). Take the data and sort into large buckets. Then sort through again and pull out common themes and concepts as subsets. Sort and review iteratively and exhaustively until every piece of information has found its place.

Another way of sorting is suggested by designer Jon Kolko as three types of actions for synthesizing insights: prioritizing, judging, and forging connections (Kolko, 2010):

- Prioritizing: by comparing pieces of data with one another, they can be ranked in importance.

- Judging: set aside those that are not relevant to the scope of the DOWE initiative and focus on those that are most relevant to the opportunity at hand.

- Forging of Connections: ascertain the relationship between different aspects of the raw data and use them as building blocks for the whole picture.

To emphasize, judging is as it is defined above: simply *determining signifi-cance*. It is not a place to impose personal opinions.

Additionally, mind maps, which are graphical representations connecting concepts or ideas, can be used to keep track of and organize the DOWE team's rationale and thought process. The graphic of DOWE's network in Chapter 3 (Figure 3.1) is an example of a mind map.

Pay attention to "extreme users" as sources of compelling insights and inspiration. They represent the attitudes that reside at polar opposites of the spectrum, bookending where everyone else exists. Extreme users delineate the boundaries of thought, inform on the distance and range between viewpoints, provide interesting intelligence for comparison's sake, and are useful for testing provocative ideas later on in the DOWE process.

Step 2. Review each pile or grouping and capture tensions, contradictions, and surprises. Construct statements in the voice of the user, in first person. Pose questions raised by the data beginning with, "How might we ...?" These are your insights. Make sure they are written down separately and organized, and verify their direct ties to the data. If stuck, take a step back, look at a grouping of information, reflect, and consider: "What's really being said here? What do all these mean?" It's a discovery process whereby insights are uncovered.

Step 3. Repeat these steps iteratively until a body of insights is created and then proceed to sort the insights to determine how they relate to one another. The number of insights you end up with could depend on the size of the research and the initiative itself. Ultimately, the collection should ade-quately represent themes and learning from user research that speak to the key influencers of the experience. Please also note that while it is possible to derive one insight from one observation, it is often (and preferable) that insights are backed up by *multiple* observations or groupings of data. Prevalence indicates *salience* in the context; that is, the more often you see something, the more likely it has greater influence.

People find insight building to be either frustrating or exhilarating or some combination of both. This wonderful tension comes from working in the complex abstract, which is no less important than the concrete. DOWE changes lives, so be persistent in your search for discoveries.

Examples of Insights

Vijay Kumar provides an example of how one goes from observation to insight. There's a picture of people sitting at small tables in an outdoor plaza. The observation is: "People so often move a chair a few inches this way or that before sitting on it." The insight from that is: "Before taking possession of things, people demonstrate their control over them as a declaration of autonomy to themselves" (Kumar, 2013, p. 139).

Again, insights are derived from patterns seen in user research, unique to every context as an expression of the people within their own organizations. While faith in the DOWE process continues to be a requirement, the examples below, derived from raw data taken across different initiatives, are offered for inspiration, not mimicry.

"We thought it was about picking the best tool, but it's really about having a toolbox to choose from."

"It's not enough to know that change is coming, I have to experience the transformation while it's happening"

"I'm supportive of change as long as I don't have to do anything different."

"On some things I want to be treated equally, and on others I want to be treated differently."

Once in a while, if a team is really lucky, one special user provides a sound bite that speaks volumes for other users and their experience, offering an insight as a gift: "I'm overpaid for what I do, but I'm underpaid for what I could do."

Using Insights

Insights are the springboard for the next steps in the DOWE process. They further build the Culture Study and are also used for validation, reframe, the provocative proposition, and the experience map (and other visuals).

The Validation and the Reframe

Insights are the first validation checkpoint for the assumptions and predictions developed up front, prior to user research. This initial work represented the DOWE team's framing. One iteration of the learning loop is completed by going back to compare whether insights have proven or disproven initial thoughts. This is also a chance for the team to learn and teach others about the gap between "what we think" and "what is." In design, this is often referred to as the "reframe." Reframe is the movement from an initial frame to another, whether from one place to another or zooming in or out (Kelley, 2005, p. 184). It's a change in perspective. If the insights are done well, they should disrupt thinking and reframe mindsets – sometimes more than once – with game-changing possibilities. Consider, for instance, a company that reframes itself from a retailer selling home goods to a connector of "like-minded strangers" who happen to have a shared interest in home design. Think about how that reframe might change business strategies, branding, marketing, and relationships to customers, attitudes, and behaviors (Sacks, 2014).

In DOWE, the reframe is based on new and in-depth understanding of the users and their experience. There are different ways to express this, but suggested formats might look like:

We thought X, but we learned Y because of insight A

Or

We used to think...we now believe...

Reframe statements are part of the ingredients that go into designing and innovating. They literally reframe views and enable the design of solutions in unprecedented ways, bringing forth potentially profound change.

The Reframe Effect

The Lost Dogs Home in Melbourne, Australia, provides a great illustration of a reframe's effect. Like all shelters, the organization had a hard time finding homes for their orphaned animals. Remarkable things happened when they shattered a common assumption – that animals are helpless and need rescuing. They moved away from an animal-centered approach, beyond a self-centered shelter approach, to a people-centered approach. Out of this reframe came an exceptionally successful adoption campaign. In The Human Walking Program, the dogs rescued city workers in need of walks. The event was scheduled to take place in a city park frequented by workers on their lunch breaks. Essentially, The Lost Dogs Home brought the shelter to the people, framing the activity as a benefit to the city workers. By the end of the campaign, every dog was adopted. It is well worth watching this delightful video online and sharing it with others (Lawson & Barrow, 17 November, 2014).

Here's the DOWE breakdown of this example: the shelter's aim was to convince people to adopt, so logically, they decided to design the experience around people, not animals. The capitalized words below are taken directly from the video:

Possible insight: We can connect city walkers and animals, who both need walking

We thought it was about: HELPLESS ANIMALS THAT NEED TO BE SAVED

We asked: MAYBE IT'S US WHO NEED TO BE RESCUED?

We learned: DOGS COULD DO THE RESCUING

Results: WE CHANGED THE WAY PEOPLE SEE SHELTER DOGS

OVER 5,000 OFFICE WORKERS WERE RESCUED

AND EVERY SINGLE DOG WAS ADOPTED

The Human Walking Program might not exist if not for the reframe, for it helped people to see new and different possibilities that previously went unconsidered. If insights yield a greater understanding of the current experience in its context, then the reframe serves to clarify the real problem or opportunity to address. In this case, the problem was not about getting dogs adopted, it was about getting people to adopt dogs. What a difference a shift can bring!

The thinking at the beginning of a DOWE initiative is reframed based on what is discovered through user research. The challenge originally identified might need revision or perhaps it may be something entirely different. Alternatively, perhaps the team confirms their original intentions, but with far greater clarity and focus. When dealing with complicated human relations, it's ok to have general ideas in the beginning that require further clarification. Taking time to do the work purposefully and meaningfully makes certain that when change happens, it is grounded in user-centered research. UNDERSTAND as part of the DOWE process is meant to gauge where a focus on the culture has the greatest benefits for the organization and its people.

I once counseled a manager who was asked to find a coach to improve his communication skills. He was told that he needed help to such a degree that he started to believe that he was a bad communicator. I got to know this person over a period of time and never had a problem understanding him. After some digging, it became clear his "communication problems" had to do with the fact that he had a different perspective than his coworkers. The resulting conflicts led to his alienation. What a waste of resources for the company if we hadn't dug deeper to discover the root cause of the problem.

Insights and reframe are DOWE's ways of digging deeper. Framing substantially influences the outcomes of DOWE. It's how the design team chooses to see the opportunities, outline the boundaries of their position, and influence what is ultimately designed. It can be equally liberating and restrictive (Kolko, 2011, p. 14), and therefore should be chosen deliberately. The disciplined iteration in DOWE brings blind spots and biases to the surface, addresses them, and opens up new possibilities and explanations. Allow the process to uncover the insights through iteration. With each loop, the picture becomes clearer.

The Provocative Proposition

Once the core design team has reoriented itself around reframe, the provocative proposition aligns the organization with a vision of *what could be*. Borrowed from Appreciative Inquiry, the provocative proposition is a thought-provoking challenge to the status quo. It gives people the opportunity to imagine the possibility of a different (improved or completely redesigned) experience. It answers the fundamental question, "What if?"

For the purposes of DOWE, a strong provocative proposition:

- Is an affirmative statement of the ideal organization, using wording stated in the present tense
- Identifies the elements needed in the future state
- Articulates the desired qualities
- Challenges/interrupts the status quo
- Grounds itself in the strengths of the organization and what works within it.

If the team gets stuck trying to create a statement from scratch, prompt with these typical Appreciative Inquiry questions and answer them in the form of a provocative statement:

- Which of the organization's strengths, or what's working well in the current experience, can provide for a successful future?

- When the organization is at its best, what makes it exciting, interesting, invigorating, motivating, and productive? What caused these desirable qualities? How can they be tied to the experience?

- It is (6 months, 1 year, 5 years) from now. This initiative has proven to be successful. What happened to get there? What were major milestones or indicators?

Or better yet, for more visual, nonlinear thinkers, Figure 5.7 can help organize thoughts into a provocative proposition.

The idea behind using provocative propositions is that we "form our world through the questions we ask," as David Cooperrider said. Asking provocative questions lets the DOWE team and its organization see things in the big picture without losing connection to the details. For example, in support of its vision and mission, a nonprofit began its provocative proposition with, "*How might we* collaborate to create profound change in our community through our people?" The provocative proposition becomes the goal of the DOWE initiative.

Figure 5.7. Provocative Proposition Chart.

Description of the Future State	Desired Qualities
Status Quo to Change	Strengths to Leverage
Draft Provocative Proposition:	

Visuals

By this point in the process, the DOWE-Rs know the culture and experiences inside and out. The rest of the organization won't be in the same place. Therefore, insights serve as the basis for visuals to convey the current state in a powerful and effective way. Notice how infographics go viral? That happens for good reason. Infographics use "data visualizations, charts, graphs, icons, illustrations and diagrams as design tools to help to make complex information easier to understand..." (Krum, 2014, p. 288). These visuals can express experiences, tell stories, communicate ideas, and elicit emotions in ways that words alone cannot.

Putting together a visual is yet another way for the DOWE team to think through their data and the experiences in the organization. What is created need not be hi-fidelity nor polished, but it does take effort to visually represent the collective understanding of the DOWE team. Begin by working with the insights, using the identified major and minor themes, and playing with analogies or metaphors that could explain the mechanisms at play.

Figures 5.8 and 5.9 are examples of infographics that depict the current states of two different organizations. Do you have a sense of their cultures based on these visuals, and could you describe it?

Figure 5.8. Culture Infographic Sample 1.

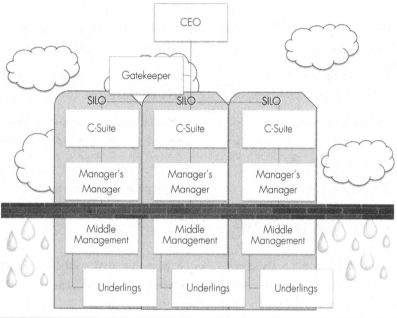

Figure 5.9. Culture Infographic Sample 2.

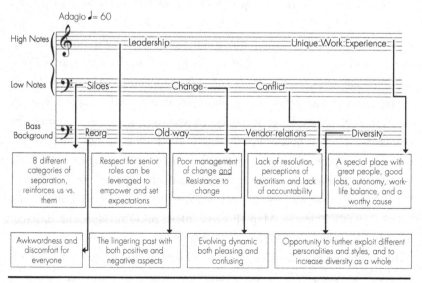

Randy Krum's book, *Cool Infographics*, offers some additional helpful tips for creating powerful visuals:

- Define a key message for the audience. This should be what viewers understand and remember after seeing the infographic (Krum, 2014, p. 283).

- Ideally, an infographic should have one clear message, and all the data visualization and illustrations support that central message (Krum, 2014, p. 283).

- More information doesn't equal better communication. Too much information can cause confusion, leaving viewers with very little understanding (Krum, 2014, p. 284).

- The design should communicate its key message in less than 5 seconds to all viewers, even those who don't take the time to read the entire infographic (Krum, 2014, p. 284).

Figures 5.8 and 5.9 are derived from a metaphor that symbolizes (brick walls and silos) and an analogy that compares (sheet music). These are two examples out of many for communicating data with impact.

An experience or journey map is another tool that can be used to represent an organization's current state and plan for the future state. Maps reflect the different phases and touch points of the experience — what happens, what engages or disengages, what's good, bad, seen, heard, touched, and felt. It deconstructs the experience into smaller pieces without disconnecting from the whole picture. A simple online search for experience maps provides many results. Some journey maps simply show the before, during, and after of the experience, while others have distinct stages mapped out. Doblin, a global innovation firm, calls it a Compelling Experiences Map. It organizes around attraction, entry, engagement, exit, and extension (Kumar, 2013, p. 179). (Note: Extension refers to what remains or sustains after the encounter.) These people-centered visuals reflect what is both real and perceived, a perspective rarely seen together in one place. Figure 5.10 is an example of an experience map based on what's been called the 5Es (Entice, Enter, Engage, Exit, and Extend) combined with sensory cues modified from Sunni Brown's Empathy Map (Brown, 2014, p. 178). Note the different touch points, which vary in number and description by project.

Keep in mind that visuals can be useful tools at any stage of the DOWE process. For example, in the early stages of a lean transformation project, a

Figure 5.10. Experience/Journey Map.

	ENTICE		ENTER	ENGAGE			EXIT		EXTEND	
TOUCHPOINTS	(1) (2)		(3)	(4)(5)(6)			(7) (8)		(9) (10)	
	Lobby downstairs	Top of the stairs	Loft entryway	Café	Loft at event start	Program/Event	Closing	Post-event	Driving Home	Long-term effect
NEEDING										
SEEING										
HEARING										
DOING										
SAYING										
FEELING										

Figure 5.11. Spaghetti Diagram (before).

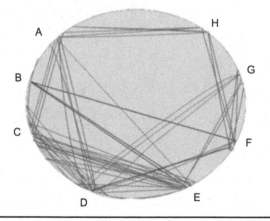

team mapped out the number of touch points in a process using what's called a spaghetti diagram. Every letter represented a different party touching a single transaction (Figure 5.11).

Figure 5.12. Spaghetti Diagram (after).

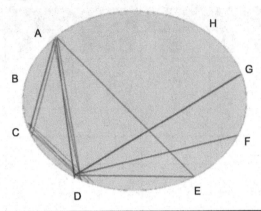

What better way to communicate a need for change? The same visual was used again after their design process to show the degree of improvement (Figure 5.12).

While the narrative provides in-depth details, references, and explanations, visuals – as demonstrated here – can be used to communicate in shorthand, with impact.

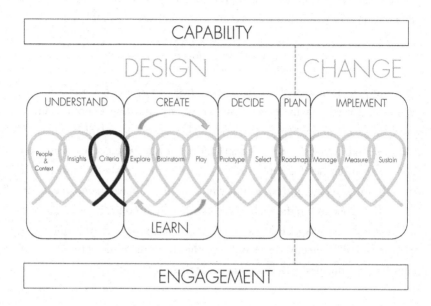

CRITERIA

<u>Input:</u> User Research Data, Insights, Culture Study, Business Strategy,

<u>Output:</u> Culture Study (Criteria and Summary)

<u>Mindset:</u>

- Think expansively and creatively.

<u>Behaviors:</u>

- Make evidence-based determinations and connections.

- Apply the wide breadth of your knowledge from user research and insight building.

- Fully and equally engage and collaborate with one another.

Right now, at this moment in the DOWE process, the team is most immersed in the existing employee experience. The knowledge acquired through user research and insight building are fresh in mind. DOWE'Rs — more than anyone else — understand the organization's culture, people, and their experiences. Now is the best time to use this expertise to establish criteria. This may feel like a disruption to the flow of the process but for good reason that will be fully appreciated when it comes to DECIDE.

Criteria Defined

Where insights synthesize learning, criteria helps to apply it. Criteria are the most critical needs for the future state, grown from a deep understanding of where things are and where they're going. They are the standard by which all strategies and designs are evaluated during *Select,* where the ideas from *Brainstorm* are chosen for implementation because they satisfy the most criteria. These measures represent the *must-have* (not the nice-to-have) *requirements* and are based on conclusions drawn between user research and the business factors.

There are two sets of criteria in DOWE. One is written from the users' perspective (i.e., the employees) and the other from the organization's standpoint (i.e., the business). Develop and treat these separately.

Importance of Criteria

Criteria combats groupthink, the tendency of teams to decide by popularity, consensus, or hierarchy ahead of quality. Those situations relinquish individual ownership for the decisions and push aside or normalize the most creative, disruptive ideas. By setting criteria, the bias in the selection process is somewhat neutralized.

The core design team's objective for setting criteria is to answer the following questions:

- What do the employees need from the experience to be successful?

- What does the organization need from its people to be successful?

Given their different vantage points, each criteria set is distinct from the other. To help the team focus, tackle one set at a time.

How to Develop Criteria

Establishing a strong set of criteria requires iteration, with each try creating a better version. First, using the inputs for reference (Figure 5.13), the team brainstorms together to exhaustively generate possible criteria. The goal is to

Figure 5.13. Establishing Criteria.

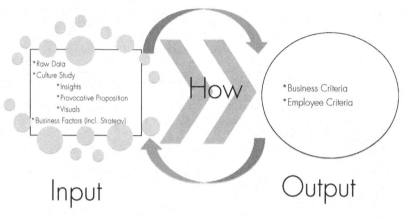

*Raw Data
*Culture Study
*Insights
*Provocative Proposition
*Visuals
*Business Factors (Incl. Strategy)

How

*Business Criteria
*Employee Criteria

Input

Output

seek the most important requirements for people and the business. The determination is easier made when there's a relative comparison against each other. They include what may be currently satisfied or lacking. Avoid the pitfall of overemphasizing the latter and taking the former for granted. For hints on brainstorming, see the next chapter.

Written in the first person, criteria shouldn't just say what, but also explain the "because" or "what for." For example: "I need clarity so I know where we are headed. Inspire me with a clear vision of the business outcomes, while empowering me to work through the anticipated ambiguity along the way." The same goes for business criteria: "The business requires alignment of objectives, behaviors, and results across the entire organization to ensure everyone's working in the same direction." Note how the business criteria is important to the organization, but not necessarily as much to its people and vice versa. They have different needs and priorities.

Explaining "why?" also helps. This challenges the team to communicate the motivation and purpose behind the criteria. For example: "We need to be constantly reminded in our understanding of the big picture because it keeps us connected to our greater purpose."

*NOTE: These examples are untethered from the context, the companies, and the teams that wrote them. They are provided here as illustrations of format only.

Figure 5.14. Organization Criteria.

Goal	• What needs to happen in order for the organization to fulfill its mission and vision? • Why is it strategically important for the organization to address those needs?
Perceptions	• What are the expectations of staff from the perspectives of the board, the community, and the markets served?
Attributes	• Are there any aspects that are conditional vs. universal in application? • Are there any processes, procedures or policies that must be changed?
Constraints	• Are there constraints in time, budget, or current state that will carry over to future state? • What are the "givens" or "can't be changed" conditions?

Source: Author's adaption of Design Criteria found in Jeanne Liedtka and Tim Olgivie's *Designing for Growth: A Design Thinking Tool Kit for Managers* (2011, p. 207).

Figure 5.15. Employee Criteria.

Goal	• What needs to happen in order for people to fulfill the organization's mission and vision? • Why is it strategically important for the organization to address those particular people needs?
Perceptions	• What expectations does the staff have of their employer?
Attributes	• Are there any aspects that are conditional vs. universal in application? • Are there any processes, procedures or policies that must be changed for people to do what's needed?
Constraints	• Are there constraints in time, work, or people needs? • What are the "givens" or "can't be changed" conditions that employees have?

Source: Author's adaption of Design Criteria found in Jeanne Liedtka and Tim Olgivie's *Designing for Growth: A Design Thinking Tool Kit for Managers* (2011, p. 207).

After the brainstorming is exhausted, check the criteria against the prompts in Figures 5.14 or 5.15 (depending on which set you're working from) and add more as needed. Then group similar concepts together and prioritize or revise.

As a constraint, narrow down to no more than 5–7 criteria for each set. This obligates the team to only select *those which are most critical*. Any less sets the bar too low and any more will be difficult to attain.

Compare this selection against the definition of criteria and eliminate accordingly:

- Only select "must haves" and eliminate "nice to haves"

- Confirm that criteria can be tied directly to conclusions drawn from user research (for employee criteria) or organizational strategy (for business criteria)

- Ensure that the criteria provides a way to evaluate and select future plans and actions

- Force rank what remains as necessary

Once you complete one set of criteria, repeat the entire process for the other set.

Note that as representatives of the business, the executive sponsors are involved with the development of business criteria, ultimately affirming what represents the most critical business needs for the initiative. This is a great opportunity to put before a steering committee or as a platform for an offsite strategy meeting facilitated by the core design team.

When finished, criteria are set aside for the time being. Again, they will be used in *Select* to narrow down which ideas or concepts to pursue. At that point, only those that best meet *both sets* of criteria will be chosen.

Experiencing UNDERSTAND

It's easy to get lost in the day-to-day activities of the DOWE process, but never forget that all this work is tied to and drives a greater purpose. As a deliverable, the Culture Study narrative is built throughout UNDERSTAND. Here's what really happens: UNDERSTAND uncovers, works with, revises, selects, and communicates the framing, which in turn drives actions. Healthy team collaboration is critical because the DOWE process requires the negotiation of multiple viewpoints into one. Once established, the Culture Study and the framing behind it are the foundation used to create the strategy and design of work experience.

Also during this time, the DOWE team goes through their own experience as they lead the process on behalf of the organization. As Tim Brown describes, design "cycles through foggy periods of seemingly unstructured experimentation and bursts of intense clarity, periods of grappling with the Big Idea and long stretches during which all attention focuses on the details. Each of these phases is different, and it's important – if only for the morale of the team – to recognize that each feels different and calls for different strategies"(Brown, 2009, p. 63).

UNDERSTAND, as the front end of the DOWE process, begins with a lot of optimism – not just your own but that of others' as well. As one DOWE-R put it, I "felt the hope and desires of our co-workers that the work we were doing would make a difference in their lives" (anonymous, personal communication, May 13, 2014). This may add pressure or it may empower, depending on the DOWE-R's personality. Keep in mind also that the beginning of UNDERSTAND also marks the beginning of the team itself. Being a new team, DOWE-Rs go through typical group formation phases of forming, storming, norming, performing (Tuckman, 1965). Familiarity, trust, and comfort levels are still in their infancies and need cultivation. This is why the scheduled team touch points are so important to keep.

Soon enough, UNDERSTAND increases in intensity. Be prepared at times to feel overwhelmed at the complexity or difficulty of the work. It's easy to get lost along the way, cognitively knowing where it will go, but not feeling it. This is natural and to be expected. Discovery is part of DOWE, and it requires time and a number of imperfect, indirect steps to get there. Thorough user research reflects how multilayered and pervasive culture in work experiences can be. Have faith that the process gets there through iteration and that other organizations have also experienced this and come out of it for the better. One DOWE-R remarked, "The DOWE experience was at first daunting, especially being a task-oriented person. But the ultimate value of the iteration process and the depth of learning created a solid platform from which to build meaningful and sustainable changes that were a natural fit in our culture." During moments of impatience or discord, take the time to reflect, allow thoughts to percolate in the background, experiment, and be persistent. Rely on strong working relationships with fellow DOWE-Rs during vulnerable times. When UNDERSTAND concludes, the team has uncovered key insights about the organization's people and context. It is ready for things to get messy again as the team moves, finally, into CREATE & LEARN.

CHAPTER 6

CREATE & LEARN

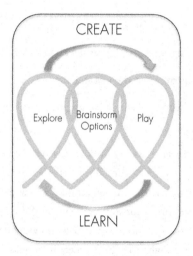

TEAM PULSE

The beginning of CREATE & LEARN is a critical check-in point for the DOWE team. Celebrate and take advantage of all the learning, successes, and progress to date. Address any remaining issues that have the potential to derail the initiative. Discuss:

- What unofficial roles have individuals on the team adopted? How are they working?

- Are changes appropriate at this time?

- Have we kept to our norms and honored promises to each other? How?

- What other norms have emerged and do we want to continue or change them?

- Is there anything that needs to be addressed in order to let go?

- What challenges or barriers have we struggled with, individually and as a team?

- Do we need help? (Never be afraid to ask for help or support.)

- Where are we strongest? How can we leverage that?

- Where can we improve? What's missing?

- Are we practicing what we are preaching and modeling the changes? In what ways?

If any team member feels strongly about an issue, then it should be raised for discussion. If a person is unsure about whether to raise a concern, they should ask themselves: "Is this an ongoing or a new pattern?"; "Will this make a difference tomorrow or any point in the future?" If the answer is yes to either of these questions, then the individual with the concern should first think through how and when it should be conveyed with diplomacy and intended impact. Then they should prepare possible responses to people's reactions or follow up questions.

Regardless of how things are going, have authentic discussions or social time together that result in a renewed and recommitted team. Now more than ever, the group must collaborate to effectively take advantage of each member's talents. Empirical research has shown that leveraging diversity only happens under the right conditions (Van Der Vegt & Bunderson, 2005), so make sure the team is in a good place to begin creating.

"THE BEST WAY TO PREDICT THE FUTURE IS TO CREATE IT."

- PETER F. DRUCKER

CREATE & LEARN OVERVIEW

CREATE & LEARN is the part of the process that some describe as stimulating and fun, while others may experience it as messy and uncomfortable. Both perspectives are accurate. It's a roller coaster ride of accelerated iteration through the learning loops, more so than anywhere else in the DOWE process. At this point, thinking diverges broadly and inhibitions are overcome to reveal new possibilities for how things *could be*, and how to get there. Here is where the creation of new experiences happens.

This phase begins where UNDERSTAND left off – and applies what was learned into the creative design process, combining it with generated ideas through play and experimentation. This, too, is another learning opportunity to use creativity to explore possible solutions. It is not designing for the sake of designing. Instead, paradigms are questioned, new possibilities arise, transformation occurs, and ideas evolve. Everybody gets something different out of this part of the process as they create, learn, iterate, and learn again – together.

There are several hallmarks of this phase. First, CREATE & LEARN is not an individual activity, it's a form of co-creation with others. It is where collaboration should be strongest and diversity yields its greatest advantages. Also expect to iterate in CREATE & LEARN. Again, iteration is the act of going through things over and over again – not repetitively, but progressively. It is a key component of how DOWE works. Every loop is a move toward getting better and better as the team moves back and forth and in-between, each iteration serving as a catalyst for something new, different, or improved. It takes stamina and persistence to go through *Explore, Brainstorm,* and *Play* (multiple times if necessary) and not get discouraged. Instead, allow each attempt to push toward continuous improvement and better outcomes.

For those who hold to "one right answer" or "get it right the first time," being comfortable with failure and iteration is counterintuitive and is thus a great development opportunity. So much has been written and said about fear of failure, to such a degree that there's a sense of agreement that the fear can be debilitating. Golden Krishna wrote about its impact on design: "Talk of failure can slow ideation and start an endless, paranoid debate when discussing the abstract ... when actually readying something for the real world, we shouldn't always rely on the intended solution. Failure is always a potential outcome, and any good system considers how to deal with that failure in an effective way ..." (Krishna, 2015, p. 205). DOWE's way is to see failure as a welcome learning opportunity, not something to be feared or permitted to stifle innovation.

People also get stuck when they are put in situations where they are expected to be creative in group settings, like brainstorming or sharing their ideas. Anxiety heightens and they become extremely self-conscious. This is a natural, but ultimately self-defeating response. DOWE-Rs are required to apply their knowledge and ingenuity toward developing ideas, solutions, and new experiences. However, sometimes negative self-talk and insecurities can give rise to misperceptions, ill-conceived actions, and self-imposed road-blocks. An open, willing, and unhindered mindset must be managed purposefully to remain energized, optimistic, and resilient.

Beyond getting past mental barriers, the trick is to just get started – somewhere, or anywhere for that matter. This is Improvisation 101. Don't judge or worry about whether it's good or bad. There will be a time for evaluation, refinement, and selection later on in the process. Improv expert Patricia Ryan Madson writes in *Improv Wisdom* that "All starting points are equally valid. They begin where they are, often in the middle .... Once a job is under way you have a new and more realistic perspective" (Madson, 2005, pp. 53–54). Take inspiration from how other creators make some-thing new – artists, innovators, groundbreaking thinkers. Talk to them, read about how they work, watch videos, or find some other way of getting motivated. Author Anne Lamont reassures, "very few writers really know what they are doing until they've done it" (Lamott, 1994, p. 22). Such is the case with DOWE. No one knows at this point of the process what will come out of it. Make peace with that, let go of the worry, and start creating.

CREATE & LEARN's deliverables include the brainstormed ideas to develop and refine for the new experiences, organized into the Strategy and Design Blueprint. Written in the latter part of this phase and extending into DECIDE, it describes the evolutionary journey and rationale for the selected options, ultimately presenting the strategy for the new experience(s) and the next steps. (See a sample outline/table of contents in the Appendix C).

As the team moves into *Brainstorm*, remember that in DOWE, there's a time and place for everything. CREATE & LEARN is not the place for lim-itations, playing devil's advocate, analyzing why it won't work, doing con-crete planning, or even asking, "Where is this going?" Again, there is a time for all of them in the DOWE process, but not here. It is *imperative* that these behaviors don't intrude upon the creative process. Doing so would be as silly as sleeping in the kitchen when you've got a bedroom. There are different spaces for good reason. Instead, relish in the unique opportunity this initiative brings: to have fun being creative while also positively impacting the future of the organization and people's lives within it.

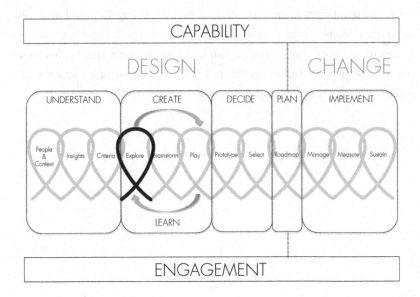

EXPLORE

Input: Anything and everything (experiences, perspectives, research, etc.)

Output: Greater knowledge, expanded minds

Mindset:

- Be open, curious, resourceful, and persistent in the search for knowledge

Behaviors:

- Thoroughly investigate generated leads

- Explore little and big ideas alike

- Engage, collaborate, and share with others to achieve more as a team

Explore is actually an activity that comes in and out throughout the DOWE process, but it is especially useful prior to brainstorming. In *Explore*, the core design team builds knowledge and inspiration by learning from everything and everywhere, hunting and gathering anything that could inform their perspective for the design challenge. It goes beyond doing primary and secondary research — it seeks stimulus to synthesize concepts and ideas. It's more than just collecting knowledge; it's laying the groundwork for knowing how and when to use it.

There are a number of ways the team can choose to *Explore*, individually or together. These can include keeping personal notebooks; sharing a physical or virtual inspiration board; having discussions with subject matter experts; engaging in casual conversations with users; going to conferences, talks, or meet ups; looking for analogies; creating mind maps; and so on. *Explore* develops capabilities and resourcefulness that only grow with practice, like mental calisthenics. Set aside time to indulge curiosity, even if it has to be scheduled. Enjoy the natural human inclination to seek information and learn.

During this time, some teams choose to create personas — user profiles/personalities comprised of a set of shared attributes that describe the various archetypes that emerged from user research (Kumar, 2013, p. 211). These are the team's interpretation of patterns they see in groupings of people. Personas have long been used in design, consumer research, and marketing. Customer "segments" can be described with personas. As a tool, they can clarify and remind the team who they're designing for, which can be a helpful aid.

However, sharing personas with the greater organization out of context for its intended use can be risky and problematic. Criticisms about their accuracy could emerge, even if they are created directly from data. Even worse, new stereotypes are introduced. Pegging individuals without their choice or agreement could cause new cultural issues, especially when it affects talent decisions (hiring, promotion, transfers, etc.) and relationships. Other examples of where misuse of personas can be destructive include calling people by their persona labels or excusing shortcomings as typical of a certain persona. The reality is that people are far more complex as individuals than any of these generalized categories. From DOWE's point of view, personas can be helpful and dangerous at the same time, so tread carefully and manage purposefully.

*This is not to say all kinds of archetypes should be avoided. An organization might decide they want to design for or develop a certain set of talent profiles and use them to create programs to build those capabilities. That's different than user personas and perfectly acceptable as a tool.

Explore work can be fun – grab anything that serves to inspire or teach. Then go beyond that to find places where cross-pollination might happen, from different fields of study to cross-functional applications, and so on. Combinations or new ideas can be found anywhere from game theory to biology to math, or even physical objects. I'll give you an example: One day, I was reading an excerpt from Penn Jillette's book in an online magazine. While talking about his experiences on *Celebrity Apprentice*, he references Daniel Kahneman's book, *Thinking Fast and Slow* and its idea of ego depletion. That reminded me to go back into this book's manuscript and make sure I remember to talk about authenticity. The topic is only tangentially related to ego depletion, but it was enough of a trigger for me to go back and improve upon my writing. This is how *Explore* works, where curiosity takes hold and roams free to spark inspiration. It is amazing (and surprising) what is found – one only needs to be open to discovery and pay attention.

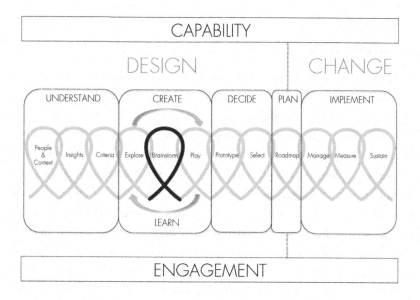

BRAINSTORM

Input: Everyone's skills, capabilities, experiences, and knowledge

Output: Many ideas, options, and/or possible designs or solutions

Mindset:

- See yourself as a capable, creative person

- Be open to listen

- Be intuitive

- Be optimistic, think in terms of possibilities

Behaviors:

- Be agile — move back and forth quickly to see the big picture and zoom in on the details

- Collaborate

- Engage and contribute

- Encourage and appreciate others for their contribution

- Focus on the present

- Pay attention

- Experiment and learn

Brainstorming has a mixed reputation. Some people love it, others dismiss it. In fact, research has shown that brainstorming doesn't always lead to better results (Mullen, Johnson, & Salas, 1991), and there are those that believe the best ideas are conceived by people working alone (Bailis, 2014). However, a major theme in DOWE is *connection* – connecting people, connecting ideas, and connecting people with ideas. Connection is a condition for innovation (Johnson, 2010), where multiple, disparate pieces catalyze when they're brought together. DOWE, which promotes the innovation of the work experience, doesn't function or happen on an individual basis. It requires the collective contribution and participation of people – people with capabilities, experiences, and knowledge to share and leverage. While working alone is great under certain circumstances, it doesn't work for this part of the DOWE process.

Brainstorming often underperforms because people underperform – as in they don't know how to do it well. Sometimes they are unpracticed and uncomfortable with the activity. Other times, politics or dysfunctional group dynamics get in the way. When done efficiently and effectively, brainstorming *can* yield good results. Think of it as a form of open innovation or as the crowdsourcing of ideas. As a methodology, it's susceptible to user error – but that doesn't mean we should discredit it wholesale. Instead, work to minimize user error and maximize the capability. This can be managed purposefully.

When a group brainstorms, participants work together to generate options, ideas, or offerings that could solve for critical needs and define or enhance a work experience. Having multiple ideas of various type and scale encourages creativity and exploration while minimizing risk. Instead of one big solution defined too narrowly, brainstorming yields many options that can be tested out in a learning environment where the stakes and repercussions are much smaller.

Creativity is a necessary precursor to innovation. Where creativity is the ability to come up with ideas, innovation connects ideas to other people, where it is shaped, adopted, and realized. In brainstorming, use creativity to enable innovation.

As was the case when building criteria, lots of ideas are encouraged to avoid the danger of having too few options at this juncture. Emile Chartier, the French philosopher, once said, "Nothing is more dangerous than an idea when it's the only one you have" (von Oech, 2008, p. 38). The act of brainstorming itself is not unlike group improvisation (McCracken, 2009, p. 135), where everyone is present, engaged with, and building off one another in the moment. Improvisation's principle of "yes, and ..." works well here. It accepts everything, implies no judgment, offers unconditional agreement, and then builds off of what someone else has offered. Disciplined brainstorms set the stage for collaborative exploration and development of ideas. They connect diverse vantage points, creating new combinations. New possibilities are considered without hindrance. Human ingenuity drives innovation. The product of *Brainstorm*, created by the empowered people of the organization, is the antithesis of prescribed solutions.

By this point, the team should be warmed up from brainstorming criteria earlier in the DOWE process. *Brainstorm* begins with curiosity, asking "What if?" and "How might we ...?" These are classic design questions, now posed for the organization and its people. There are lots of different ways to brainstorm, and the ideas shared here are by no means exhaustive. No matter the approach, strike a balance between freedom and structure to encourage creativity with purpose in order to achieve real change toward the desired work experience.

"Devil's advocate" thinking ruins brainstorming and functions as a form of censorship. *Don't even think about failure.* Keep this popular Internet meme in mind: "What would you do if you knew you could not fail?" There will be a time for judging, but again, not here. DOWE team members should hold themselves and others to this expectation. Nothing shuts down the virtues of brainstorming faster than fixating on what can't work and why.

Setup and Warm Up

A proper setup precedes a great brainstorm. First, pick a time and place to bring people together. Select an adequate timeframe that adds a dose of healthy pressure to discourage wastefulness. If possible, schedule the brainstorm across two contiguous days, or perhaps one full day split in half across two days. Having the overnight spawns and percolates new ideas and allows for reflection. Next, ensure the physical space is conducive to the act of creating. Since the built environment influences behaviors, find a place free from distractions. Bring in elements that encourage flow (as defined in Chapter 3). The space should feel open. Furniture, props, and supplies should be movable and in working order. Make different mechanisms available to capture and collect the ideas (post-its, idea sheets, flip charts, wall space, markers, timer). Prepare anything else people need to be creative and inspired (food, inspiration boards, mood music, fidget toys, warm up exercises, and so on).

In addition, participants need to clear mental space. Distractions, competing priorities, and other barriers are removed so that people can be engaged and present for *Brainstorm*. Again, the magic in DOWE is how it connects the individual to others, making extraordinary things happen. Therefore, set an expectation for collaboration. Call out and eliminate anything that causes interference so people can move forward.

There are "rules" to brainstorming that guide the activity and encourage the kind of productivity that results with potentially useful ideas. Without them, there's a risk of degenerating the session with unstructured discussion (Brown, 2009, p. 78). The guidelines below, shared by Stanford's d.school, were likely learned collectively through practical experience:

- Capture All Ideas

- Defer Judgment

- Build Off the Ideas of Others

- Be Visual

- Wild Ideas Welcome!

- One Conversation at a Time

- Headline

- Go for Quantity

- Sort Similar Concepts into Clusters

The most important rule of them all is to "treat the brainstorm as an exploration, not a search" (Stanford d.school, 2009)." This isn't a hunt for answers, but an exploration of the terrain. These guidelines should be shared, discussed, and aligned up front to elicit behaviors for good brainstorming.

Some organizations need to formally and explicitly grant "permission" for people to feel comfortable and empowered to create. Do what sets the conditions for a robust brainstorm. This might come by establishing meeting norms, demonstrating brainstorming behaviors by example, setting an oath/promise/social contract with participants, providing executive encouragement, or having practice exercises and test runs.

Who participates in the brainstorm depends on your organization and how the DOWE initiative was setup. It's important to think through getting the right people in the room because they have the knowledge you need and a huge influence on the outcomes. There are several ways to structure participation. The DOWE team can take a first run at it themselves by appointing a few core design team members to lead the discussion. If they are better off participating with others in the room, a facilitator or their DOWE coach could prove helpful. Others outside the core DOWE team who have unique outlooks or influence may also participate so long as politics aren't involved. In other words, don't include executives in order to curry favor or pick some people and exclude others arbitrarily or unfairly. If the organization practices Appreciative Inquiry (as mentioned in chapters 3 and 5), the brainstorm might happen in the context of an Appreciative Inquiry summit, where many if not all people can contribute. Some organizations have invited people with certain diverse expertise, while others have set up brainstorming as a design challenge or competition. There are many different ways to brainstorm – don't be afraid to experiment with a few and see which works best.

When the gathering begins, a warm-up exercise often proves constructive. Improvisation's *I am a Tree*, for example, is great for groups of all different types and sizes. The modified version that I like to use lines people up or gathers them in a circle. A single person at the end of the queue or in the middle of the circle starts with the declaration, "I am a tree." At the same time, this person gestures or acts out what they are saying. In this case, they are standing with arms held widely above their head. They stay where they are. In sequential or random order (whatever your preference), the next person declares an adjacent idea of their own and acts it out. For example, "I am the person under the tree, reading a book." The two people remain in their poses. A third person enters with another idea. "I am the bird flying up in the sky, looking for worms." At this point, the first person may return to the group and a fourth person goes next so that three people are always in play. The pattern repeats itself at a rapid pace until everyone's had at least two turns. *I am a Tree* gets the creative juices flowing and practices improvisation behaviors that are good for brainstorming. It gets people to build off others' ideas spontaneously. It doesn't allow for preparation, but rather keeps the focus on what's immediately in front of people. Self-consciousness is discouraged, and colleagues begin to trust each other more. The occasional humor relaxes people and dissipates tension. Attention is given by a captive audience. In essence, this exercise is a human mind map, brainstormed by the participants.

The Brainstorm

The most obvious place to start the actual brainstorm is with your DOWE initiative's provocative proposition, posed in the form of "How Might We ...?" Follow up with a series of other inquiries that stimulate idea generation. For some, a blank flip chart or sheet of paper can be an intimidating start. Some groups have started with a series of open-ended questions structuring the brainstorm. Keep in mind that it is critical to remain broad to avoid dictating direction. For example, one organization's DOWE initiative was to create a culture that reflected their values so they created mindmaps beginning with each value at the center (Figure 6.1).

Another brainstorming exercise sets up parallel working, defined by *Design Thinking* author Nigel Cross as "keeping design activity going at many levels simultaneously (Cross, 2011, p. 74)." In other words, the team works on all different parts of one connected experience or solution at the same time. It offers flexibility to explore different tangents while remaining connected to the bigger picture. Try filling out a wall-sized experience/journey map for the future state. Use parallel working to design every aspect of the experience: the attraction, entry, engagement, exit, and extension. Remember, the aim is to design for an experience whereby the determination is made for the presence *or the absence* of certain conditions to support success.

The evolutionary path ideas take through the course of *Brainstorm* never ceases to amaze, like how one idea starts out as an employee newsletter and ends up being a communication channel employees can access anytime, or how the establishment of a gift shop selling company paraphernalia led to a discussion about developing a new employer brand.

Figure 6.1 Brainstorm Mindmap.

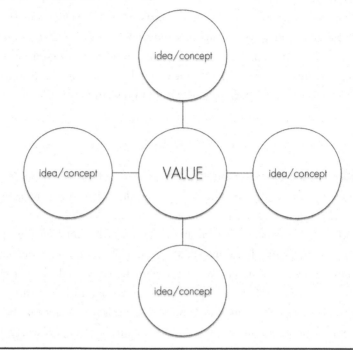

In a DOWE brainstorm, people tend to come up with lots of ideas for actions, such as things to do or programs to develop. While those are encouraged, don't forget to take the opportunity to come up with other types of ideas, such as the making of physical artifacts or a built environment that supports cultural or behavioral change. These are physical proof that "intangible" concepts, like culture, are real. Capture emotional states, psychological needs fulfilled, or sensory elements as outcomes, knowing that they can be planned against later on in the DOWE process. Also think of seizing opportunities where DOWE can piggyback, enhance, or integrate into other activities or existing practices and programs. What is it that people already know how to do well, and how can it be leveraged as a strength or capability? Don't be afraid to challenge co-designers to further explore new concepts or push boundaries. Prompt each other with "tell me more." Ask questions. Practice active listening and suggest adjacent or connecting concepts. At this stage, all ideas are equally important and valid. Don't waste time in debates or arguing the virtues of anyone's ideas, just make sure they are put out there and captured.

This is serious brain work. If fatigue starts to set in, participants should feel comfortable calling for an unscheduled group break to reset or refresh the mind as needed. Planned breaks are opportunities to bring in an unrelated activity, like jumping jacks or yoga stretches. Shifting to a distraction sometimes releases new ideas, seemingly out of nowhere.

Potential Pitfalls

Brainstorming can be uncomfortable. For some people, this discomfort can lead to frustration. It is important to acknowledge when this is happening. Explore why and address how to get back on track. It might mean reviewing the process, the provocative proposition question, the initiative's purpose statement again, or simply raising the discussion. By outing it, avoidance is made impossible. Issues are addressed and ultimately resolved. A participant once spoke on behalf of the group: "We never go big and then small and then big again – we aren't used to that." Calling this out meant that people could shift their attention away from the diagnosis (and the worry that comes with it) and on to the cure. In this case, it was getting more practice and becoming comfortable with brainstorming.

Anxieties aside, other pitfalls come from self-limitation: not pushing enough, not being creative, not coming up with new or disruptive ideas, editing or preventing wild ideas from flourishing. In one session, the participants reused past ideas without changing anything. They also had a lot of ideas with no impact – their solutions and ideas didn't reflect the excitement of their vision. As a result, they had to go back and brainstorm again.

Going the distance requires people to challenge themselves and encourage others to do the same. Ask people to elaborate on their ideas, take them to a different level (either bigger picture, or more specific), look for analogies or metaphors, combine ideas, or move them to a new application. This is tough – it demands self-motivation and persistence to keep at it, even when discouraged. After some prompting, someone once admitted, "I know what you are saying and I understand it, but I can't do it myself." Admitting this frustration got the group to pause, acknowledge where it was coming from, and then give and get encouragement to try again. Sometimes it comes down to a matter of people's lack of confidence in their ability to create. This is a mental block in and of itself and should therefore be dealt with and removed. A nurturing environment with a focus on learning helps people feel safe to experiment with not only new ideas, but also new behaviors.

Finishing Brainstorm

If allowed, brainstorms could go on forever – similar to the way overanalysis leads to paralysis. Like the rest of the DOWE process, the act of brainstorming is a series of progressive and open learning loops that eventually draw toward a conclusion. Knowing when a brainstorm is finished is a matter of balancing out "satisficing" (being ok with good enough) and "maximizing" (striving for perfection), between settling for mediocrity and expecting too much (Schwartz et al., 2002). Move on when the group collectively feels like there is a good quantity and quality of ideas *overall*. (Remember, no judgment here of individual ideas). Determine whether "flow" was achieved – was everyone engaged and at their best? If so, then move on. If any uncertainty remains, try again or see how the ideas hold up through *Play*, the next loop of the process.

This isn't about "we did this already and we're good," it's about trying again and doing better with each iteration. There should be no angst about revisiting discussions; simply try again if necessary. At any point of the DOWE process (including *Brainstorm*), don't be afraid to go back to any learning loop when there is good reason to. It will be worth the hassle to improve the quality of your results.

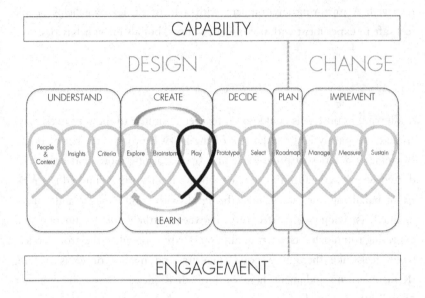

PLAY

Input: Unorganized, brainstormed ideas

Output: Familiarity with and refinement of ideas

Mindset:

• Opportunistic

• Positive and optimistic

• Playful

• Creative

Behaviors:

• Collaborate

• Connect

• Experiment and play

• Reflect and learn

You might wonder why *Play* is necessary as part of the DOWE process. Recall that the only way to develop insights during UNDERSTAND was to gain intimacy with the user research and data. In the same way, *Play* builds assuredness in ideas. Creative play comes forth through purposeful action. Including it in the DOWE process guarantees that it happens. For those that are eager or impatient to move on to decision making or planning, trust in the process is (again) required.

Play puts ideas "through the wringer" and adds substance to the ethereal. Ideas are explored through play, but not in a deficit-driven way (good vs. bad, and why things can't work). Rather, DOWE-Rs tinker and experiment with ideas to see how they work or how they might be modified to work.

Children have the natural instinct to play. They aren't taught to play, they simply play. As adults, much of that playful spirit is minimized or relegated exclusively to hobbies or extracurricular activities. As odd as it may seem to some, play at work supports innovation. Tim Brown calls it "serious play": "… exploring the world with our hands, testing out ideas by building them, role playing, and countless other activities are all natural characteristics of children at play" (Brown, 2009, p. 222).

If you haven't seen Tom Wujec's TED Talk video (Ted.com, 2010) on the Marshmallow Challenge or seen it in action, I highly recommend it. Without going into the details and spoiling it, many groups (including CEOs) have gone through it. The one group that outshines all others in this task are children. What differentiates them is their ability to play collaboratively. This is an advantage they have over adults when it comes to solving problems. The genius of play can be applied for the betterment of business performance – you just have to know how.

This learning loop begins with the big pile of ideas that came out of brainstorming. Now it's time to play.

Sort and Organize

The first thing is to organize the ideas and see how they relate to one another, especially if they were collected without any structure. This should be familiar territory for the DOWE team since it is reminiscent of insight-building activities. Go through a series of sorts until the ideas become familiar. There are many ways to do this. One way is to sort them into buckets —big ideas into big buckets and little ideas into little buckets. Consolidate duplicates and reword vague ideas for clarity.

Other ways to sort ideas are by persona or by topic. The possibilities are endless. The essence of this work is to explore and understand the ideas more thoroughly using play as a learning mechanism. The team discovers how some of the ideas might be related, how they can play off of one another, and where there might be some gaps. The physical act of sorting and organizing very easily demonstrates where the team was exhaustive and where it was not. It might be worth discussing why this is the case. Is it a topic no one wants to touch, a "wicked problem" (Buchanan, 1992, p. 15) that intimidates? Or is it not as big (or as important) as once thought? Maybe it was just a fluke or oversight and there's a need to go back and brainstorm a bit more. During the sorting and organizing, ask questions around the ideas and challenge each other to elaborate. Also think of ways to springboard off the ideas and apply them in different ways.

Serious Play

Next, get down to the business of "serious play." Play here is both a form of learning and creativity in practice. More and more is learned as DOWE-Rs work the ideas and with that they change, evolve, or connect differently into something new.

Again, there are many ways to accomplish this, but be sure to accommodate different lenses or ways of looking at the ideas without judgment. Allow minds to do some gymnastics and consider ideas from different angles. Start with the big buckets or the big ideas and go from there. Or start anywhere.

Playing with ideas can include role play, scenario testing, or storytelling to get additional insights. These exercises keep the focus on the employee-centered point of view and prevents distraction from inconsequential details (Brown, 2009, p. 94). They also help to persuasively present these ideas later on in the process. Take turns explaining or describing the ideas and compare and contrast them with others. Keep in mind this doesn't concern debate or advocating the merits of ideas, it is purely an exploration. Some ideas may be better understood visually. Pick up a pencil along with scratch paper and draw away.

I've created a deck of cards that I playfully call "the stimulus package," which was adapted from numerous sources ranging from personal knowledge to life experiences to Von Oech's Whack Pack (von Oech, 2003). It is included in Appendix D and can be used as prompts to look at ideas from different perspectives inside and out, backwards and forwards, upside down and around. Randomly pick some out, apply them to some of the ideas, and see where they go. Here are some examples that will help you play:

- Make a wish list for the issue or idea

- Change the starting point or work backwards

- How do you reframe your idea or issue in an opportunistic, strengths based, or positive way?

- Put two polar opposite concepts, issues, or ideas together to create an oxymoron

- What is the root cause of the issue? What is that root cause's root cause?

Look for each idea's unintended benefits. Some of these may be discoverable, others may emerge later on during the CHANGE portion of the DOWE process. What is found here further refines and strengthens ideas. The Apple iPhone's Siri feature offers a great example of an unintended benefit for users. Mothers of autistic children have discovered that Siri can do more than get information. It can also converse with their kids, gets them to practice enunciation, and even teaches etiquette (Newman, 2014). People don't buy iPhones expressly because it works well with autistic children, but discovering that it does is delightful. When it comes to designing experiences and other culture work, unintended benefits can manifest themselves as employee-driven passion projects, the adoption of new behaviors, or a novel use for an idea – all of which are worthy of further exploration, especially if there are willing volunteers.

As part of *Play*, also check for blind spots that could make the difference when it comes to success and failure. The invention of the phonautograph illustrates the "farsightedness and myopia" of an overlooked blind spot: its creator, Édouard-Léon Scott de Martinville, figured out a way to capture and record sound waves 20 years before Edison's phonograph. Alas, he was "hamstrung by one crucial – even comical – limitation. He had produced the first sound-recording device. But he neglected to include playback" (Johnson, 2014). This demonstrates one reason why DOWE, as with many innovations, relies on the capability and engagement of a team. Together in *Play*, a team improves ideas in ways an individual cannot. Remember at this stage, nothing should be discounted or eliminated. Playing with blind spots simply identifies what should be addressed as a way of improving ideas.

Indeed, *Play* reveals gaps and opportunities to pursue with what comes out of *Brainstorm*. This is especially true if boundaries weren't stretched enough. If there are more old ideas than new, go back to *Brainstorm* and try again. This is critical. It is better to go back now than to see the *Select* loop send you all the way back to *Brainstorm* for another round of *Play* and *Prototype*. Or worse, the organization implements something that has lost sight of the people and the purpose it was designed for – and it's the same old stuff everyone's seen before. Keep the provocative proposition top of mind as inspiration and let it guide and fuel innovation.

EXPERIENCING CREATE & LEARN

The relationships on the DOWE team have come a long way. The shared experience of UNDERSTAND and the work that went into cultivating team dynamics should be paying off. By now, as one DOWE-R described it, there's a realization of how "mutual respect and understanding of each other" can make the "difference between successful and ok vs. superb and excellence" on the team and in the outcomes (anonymous, personal communication, May 13, 2014).

As CREATE & LEARN gets underway (especially as a new skill set), the health of the DOWE team supports the churn that accompanies hard work. Angst or frustration may show itself in at least two ways. The first is in getting used to practicing creativity as a previously underutilized skill. Where people may be accustomed to being confident in their own abilities, developing and trying new skills may take some getting used to. Mental blocks may get in the way. Iteration may be required to push thinking further. People may lose patience with trying and trying again, but they must keep going. Eventually, they realize, it gets easier and better.

Losing sight of where the initiative is going is another frustration that can appear at different times in the process, depending on the person. Feeling lost causes anxiety, which can distract people from the task at hand. Mindfulness and purpose are temporarily forgotten. Doubt begins to predict the outcome, and whatever is feared the most comes to pass. In those moments, pause to discuss and work through the issues as necessary, reorient in the DOWE model and refocus on the activity in earnest. Take comfort in knowing the act of creation is difficult, and even the most talented artists struggle from time to time.

Norman Rockwell, the prolific and iconic American painter of the 20th century, felt thinking up ideas was "the hardest work" and on occasion found himself out of ideas. He had a ritual for addressing his lapses in creativity, forcing himself to brainstorm and purposely toy with bad ideas. He would go to bed discouraged. The next day, he would dig through the mess and find something salvageable, something that inevitably revealed itself to be a pretty good idea. He wrote, "I never saw an idea happen or received one ... I had to beat most of them out of my head or at least maul my brain until something came out of it. It always seems to me that it was like getting blood from a stone except, of course, that eventually something always came" (Rockwell, 1988, p. 201). He went on, "Each time, as I reached the point where I felt I was finished, at the end of my rope, I've managed to right myself. Always by simply sticking to it, continuing to work though everything seemed hopeless and I was scared silly" (Rockwell, 1988, p. 270).

Anne Lamott's "Shitty First Drafts" provides encouragement. She lets us in on the secret: "All good writers write them. This is how they end up with good second drafts and terrific third drafts" (Lamott, 1994, p. 21). What about the insecurity and sense of malaise? They feel it too. "... Nor do they go about their business feeling dewy and thrilled" (Lamott, 1994, p. 22). Despite this, writers write on, learning to "... eventually let myself trust the process – sort of, more or less" (Lamott, 1994, p. 25).

As individuals or as a team, figure out ways to get unstuck through trial and error. Try and try again. Persist. If it still doesn't work, take a break. To use a sports reference, call an "audible" at any time and ask, "Why are we not energized? Why are we stuck?" Reframe the questions and look at things from different angles, and if it still doesn't work, take another kind of break: Go for a walk. Doodle. Reflect. Read. Play a game. The brain continues to think in the background, and somehow, eventually, a breakthrough happens. Being stuck is like a quiz where everyone knows the answer; all that's left is to work through it. That 99% perspiration and 1% inspiration, or the thing that's worth doing well, is right in front of you.

As the team progresses through *Play*, begin drafting the Strategy and Design Blueprint document. At this point prior to *Select*, summarize the experience of the brainstorm process and describe *Play*. More will come in the next phase, DECIDE.

CHAPTER 7

DECIDE

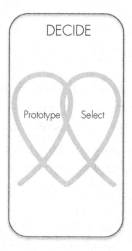

DECIDE OVERVIEW

How are decisions made in your organization? Ever been stuck or over-whelmed because you don't know what to do? Have you disagreed with others about decisions in the past? What caused the discord and how was it resolved? How about the best decisions you ever made or were a part of? What made them great and why? What role did good or bad luck play in the outcomes?

Chances are the answers to these questions vary. Many decision models attempt to add consistency, structure the thought process, and limit irratio-nal thinking. Still, many good and bad organizational decisions today are made by a select few (if not one) — individual(s) whose power is granted by job title or political influence. Other business decisions are made based on predictable knowledge; deciding x will result in y, which leads to z. Flow charts are great visual examples of these types of decisions. Budget allocation is another example: if you fund x, y happens. If you don't fund x, y will not happen. Outcomes are mostly black and white. Still there are others who prefer to rely on data to determine choices. Decisions about people and culture are different than other business decisions. People are an unpredictable and variable factor. That means that when it comes to people-related decisions, the path chosen is based on the highest *probability* of achieving the intended outcome. Hence, the need to UNDERSTAND so thoroughly.

DECIDE is yet another example of where the DOWE approach is different. Like everything else in the process, comprehensive, purposeful consideration is employed. The previously established employee and business criteria, which may feel like so long ago, began the path toward decisions. Everything else since then, *Explore, Brainstorm, Play,* and the upcoming *Prototype* and *Select*, provide learning that support the team's choices for the new experience.

If the organization has its own decision-making models or philosophies, these can be accommodated as the team thinks through the options, perhaps as part of *Play* or *Prototype*. They may help build the case for one option over the other or provide an additional opportunity for research and analysis. However, the DOWE process itself will be the ultimate decision-making tool when it comes to which options to pursue. How this works will be discussed in greater detail when it comes to *Select*.

Whatever history, baggage, or inclinations the team may have about past decisions, good or bad, it's critical at this point to approach DECIDE with an openness to choosing in a whole new way. This may prove difficult for some people. They have their biases, they like their own ideas. Focus on this: DECIDE is just another part of the process. To accept DOWE is to commit to its approach, including how decisions are made.

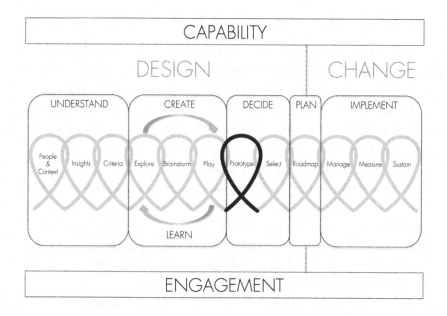

PROTOTYPE

Input: Organized, brainstormed ideas

Output: Learnings from prototypes and pilots

Mindset:

- Open-mindedness that avoids preconceived notions

- Optimism

- Organization and planning

- Curiosity and learning

Behaviors:

- See things from different angles and incorporate them into your thinking

- Pay attention all around

- Collaborate and engage with teammates and users

- Try different things

- Create and plan for interesting interactions where everyone learns

Out of *Play*, there will be some ideas that need prototyping. *Prototype* is another form of exploration. Its purpose is to further refine ideas and gather intelligence for the decision making that comes next in *Select*. Prototypes are lo-fidelity mock-ups, small-scale pilots, or experiments that inform on how the ideas might function "in the real world" or how they might scale up. It's where multiple versions of minimum viable products can be compared.

Prototyping is a soft entry into DECIDE — it is another iteration toward the decision-making process, but feels like an extension of *Play*. Those eager to move to on to *Select* must give this learning loop proper dedication. What may feel like a forced delay is actually testing out the brainstormed ideas, getting answers about how they work sooner rather than later and evaluating their merits *prior* to decision making (Brown, 2009, p. 89). Figure 7.1 shows how one organization presented plans for *Prototype*.

There are a number of benefits to *Prototype*. First, it's another chance to build engagement with the user base that volunteered to participate in the initiative, including executive sponsors as equal (not greater) stakeholders. Use this opportunity to invite new participants who may have just joined the organization or those who have since developed an interest in the work. Together, these employees make up the test groups or pilots that evaluate

---

Figure 7.1. Example of Prototype.

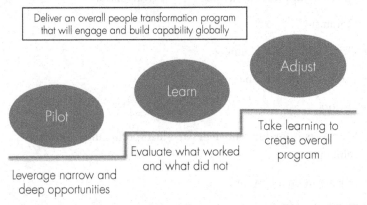

ideas and other prototypes from different vantage points, further refining the options through the lens of "How might we make this work?" and "How might we simplify for greatest impact?" Adjustments improve the ideas and mitigate risk at the same time by revealing various dynamics or blind spots, thus preventing unwelcome surprises later on. This is an important contribution toward the decision making process, so be sure to collaborate with the users as true co-creators. With sufficient efforts dedicated to *Play* and *Prototype*, DOWE-Rs prepare for *Select* by learning their way there.

There are many ways to prototype, so select the approaches best suited for the initiative. The prototypes and pilots should:

- Communicate the experimental nature of these activities, emphasizing that no final decisions have been made. Highlight that employees' participation will significantly influence the eventual decisions.

- Gather perspectives from across the organization, by persona or demographic if applicable.

- Utilize different types of interactions with what's being tested (how people learn it, share it, use it in various ways, etc.).

- Offer insights that the team wouldn't otherwise have, with resulting actions and follow up.

Before moving on, remember to collect all the ideas, even those where prototype or pilot were not necessary. Then get ready for some decisions in *Select*.

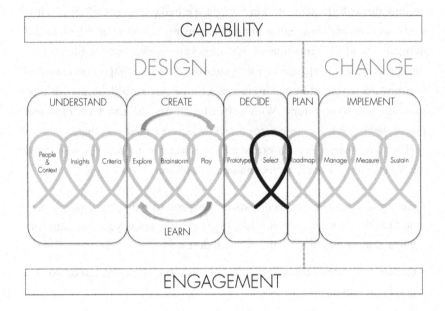

SELECT

Input: Learning from prototypes and pilots, organized brainstormed ideas

Output: Selected idea(s) and/or design(s), organized into a holistic strategy

Mindset:

• Open-mindedness

• Impartial judgment

Behaviors:

• Engage

• Collaborate

• Discern

Constraints

As the team moves into *Select*, those eager for resolution can celebrate. This is where decisions are finally made to determine the overall strategy and design (or combination of designs). DOWE's selection process is never based on personal preferences, bias, popularity, or comfort level. Instead, *Select* is achieved through the comparison of ideas against three constraints: What is viable? What is possible? Which ideas best satisfy both sets of criteria? To explain:

- What is *viable* indicates what works consistently and reliably. It also selects for ideas that elicit the intended behaviors and results *in most cases*.

- What is *possible* delineates what is within the realm of possibility and can be implemented.

- *What best satisfies both sets of criteria* refers only to that which meet both business and employee criteria. The more criteria met, the more likely the idea should be considered. Doing this secures the tie back to the context, including user research and business factors.

In Figure 7.2 the space that satisfies all three constraints are options (whether they are experiences, ideas, designs, programs, actions, artifacts, and so on) to pursue. Those selected become part of the overall strategy for the designed experience.

Figure 7.2. Constraints.

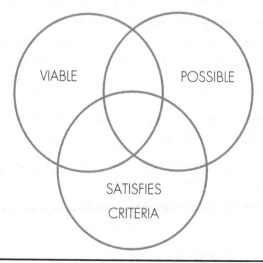

Constraints are used by designers as tools to add structure, challenge, and rigor to their design process. Sometimes they're brought in during brainstorming or idea generation. For DOWE, constraints are primarily a decision-making tool, one that helps the team learn how their options measure up against them. There is a conscious choice with DOWE to delay the introduction of constraints until now, mostly because people are prone to premature convergence, self-limitation, and other types of narrow thinking when it comes to work experiences and culture. Recall that during CREATE & LEARN, idea generation encouraged possibilities with no limitations as a way to challenge the status quo and to innovate. By the time the process arrives at DECIDE, options that advanced, developed, and matured through *Play* and *Prototype* are ready to be evaluated against constraints.

Using Constraints

Some teams take all three constraints at once, while others choose to sort options through each lens. They all arrive at the same point, so take the path that is most appropriate for the DOWE team. For larger design teams, each sort can be split into breakout discussions for each lens, and then brought back together for further discussion as a group.

In the rare, yet-to-be-seen, but possible scenario where constraints eliminate all the options, the team may loop back to *Brainstorm* using the constraints and compare/contrast between the two sets of ideas. Creativity should never be stifled regardless of whether constraints are included or not.

If a large number of options remain *after* constraints, additional filters may be used to trim down the selection. Here are some suggestions:

• Ranking based on readiness in the organization

• Amount of time or effort required — with the aim to prioritize the smallest actions with the greatest impact

• Investment value — greatest bang for buck (note: making choices based solely on cost doesn't work — value is key)

• Scale: the degree the option impacts at an individual, team, or organizational level

• By company values (if they are a part of the equation)

Look at the options and answer the following questions: What remains? Are these disruptive enough to make a tangible difference? How do they relate to one another? Can they be sequenced? Integrated simultaneously? How can they be arranged and connected to one another?

Next, look for unintended consequences and make adjustments as necessary. Unintended consequences are flaws or mechanisms in the design that have negative implications. These can create inconsistencies, prevent change, and even cause the initiative to fail (Harris & Ogbonna, 2002, p. 32). Expect to discover and confront additional unintended consequences when CHANGE is executed, but take time to identify and solve for as many potential pitfalls as possible, preemptively.

The last call of Superbowl XLIX is an example of an unintended consequence. Seattle Seahawks' coach Pete Carroll decided to pass the ball instead of running it in. The play was intercepted by the New England Patriots, giving them the win with a final score of 28–24. "It's the worst result of a call ever," Carroll said. "The call would have been a great one if we'd caught it. It would have been just fine and nobody would have thought twice about it. We knew we were going to throw the ball one time in the sequence somewhere, and so we did, and it just didn't turn out right" (The Today Show, 2015). Despite well-laid plans, Coach Carroll and his team fell victim to *what else could happen.*

Take the selected options and ponder as many results as possible for "what else could happen?" Consider the residual impacts on the system, as discussed in Chapter 2, where changes in one place could show up elsewhere. Use the Burke–Litwin Model (as explained in Appendix F) as an aid. Try to find, design, and plan for these foreseen consequences. Look for common unintended consequences in organizations such as actions or activities ritualized into meaningless routines, hijacking by other agendas (political, personal, or otherwise), erosion of the culture by contradictory messages, events, or interactions, and the reinvention of the culture as a cover for sustaining the old ways (Harris & Ogbonna, 2002, p. 45). Think about long-term implications, the emergence of new problems, possible precedents that cannot be sustained, and undesirable behaviors or reactions. This point in the DOWE process eliminates certain unintended consequences, but it can't prevent or predict everything. It is important to be aware of them so a response can be anticipated and prepared. If addressed promptly, unintended consequences, or the failures that can come with them, are recoverable learning opportunities.

Consider the selected options as a whole. Use sticky notes or a mindmapping tool to organize and sequence them into an overall strategy and/or design. Is there a format that elegantly reflects the design in one place? Would an experience map serve this purpose? Regardless of what you use, document the journey to selection and how the ideas and overall design relate and support one another. How do the components come together to create an overall desired experience? Has the status quo been challenged? Does the overall strategy and design have impact? If the answer is "no" or "not sure," then fix it. Go back as far as necessary in the DOWE process to answer these questions. Revisit the Culture Study narrative and reanchor on business factors, user research, key insights, reframe, and criteria. If the team can answer yes to these questions, then it becomes a matter of record in the Strategy and Design Blueprint.

Once the Blueprint is ready, a major milestone is achieved. Share it with executive sponsors to ratify for the next phase of the DOWE process, CHANGE. Though feedback should be welcome and considered, recall that the sponsors agreed to delegate leadership of the design to the DOWE team, that there were ample opportunities for co-creation and that decisions on the design have already been made. Remember also that from the earliest stages of the DOWE process, organizational ambition for the initiative was established up front. The boldness of the Strategy and Design Blueprint should not be in question at this point. Executive sponsors must be willing to fulfill their commitment to "accept and support the design outcomes recommended by the team, with the knowledge that decisions are made with employee and business needs in mind," per the initial DOWE Agreement.

There is one more thing to DECIDE. Those involved in the initiative – the DOWE-Rs, their users, and their leaders have to decide whether to *personally* commit to the Strategy and Design Blueprint and the CHANGE that will come with it. DOWE is not a "one and done" task to finish and then move on. The resources and effort invested in the DOWE process will be wasted if people don't see it through. The commitments need to begin with those who designed it. A commitment is a promise, purposefully made to be meaningful and have impact. It is each individual's oath to satisfy a role in the implementation of the design and/or strategy. This formal pledge is shared with others so that all can support and encourage one another to be

(1) accountable and (2) deliver on their promises. Not to be taken lightly, this is everyone's buy-in. Format isn't important as long as commitments are made to take action and they are included in the Strategy and Design Blueprint. See the Appendix E for a sample template.

EXPERIENCING DECIDE

Where CREATE & LEARN made the DOWE team's thinking broad and divergent, DECIDE added depth to the generated ideas and eventually converged with *Select*. It brings the question, "How might we...?" to resolution. Finally having answers makes this some people's favorite point in the DOWE process. That the team had to work so hard to get here makes this even sweeter.

Having healthy DOWE team dynamics in the background of decision making builds greater confidence in the outcomes. One DOWE-R had this to say about it: "The process is mostly fun, but even when difficult, it keeps moving along without resentments and adversarial relationships among participants, which I wouldn't have thought possible. And that helps the team feel better about one another and the results they've designed in the end" (anonymous, personal communication, September 25, 2017). The trust built on the team affords members the "confidence to not always agree for good reason," as another DOWE-R described it, and to have meaningful discussions to reconcile different points of view (anonymous, personal communication, May 13, 2014).

With the help of impartial constraints, decisions can be made with confidence against an agenda that is both people- and business-centered — and untainted by anyone else. Once the selection decisions are made and all possible foreseen consequences accounted for, it is the expectation that everyone on the DOWE team (and their executive sponsors) gets behind it, as if it were their own personal decision. It is after all, a conclusion that is co-created and thus co-owned. There are still plenty of challenges ahead, and they must be faced from a place of strength. Touch base with each other to ensure that this is the case and address any remaining issues now.

Finalize the Strategy and Design Blueprint document with a narrative of the journey to the selected options, along with a graphical summary that may be used as a communication device during CHANGE. Now that the organization has determined *what* it will do, the DOWE-Rs must see to *how* it will be realized through PLAN and IMPLEMENT.

CHAPTER 8

PLAN

*NOTE: If organizational change management is a new or developing capability for any DOWE-Rs, or if there's interest in understanding the conceptual background behind DOWE's approach to CHANGE, please review the extensive Change Primer in the Appendix F as a team.

PLAN OVERVIEW

DOWE-related CHANGE is different from any previous change efforts. To begin with, the Strategy and Design Blueprint was created from a deep understanding of the context and its people. It's a solution created just for them. Given that the intent of DOWE is to innovate, the Strategy and Design Blueprint to be implemented is a game changer that will require a certain degree of transformation to achieve any sense of permanence. The next phase, IMPLEMENT, is a form of organizational change. PLAN will prepare for this by determining what needs to be learned, how people need to be engaged, and what communication needs to happen for individuals, teams, and the entire organization before, during, and after the change. Using their knowledge of the employees, DOWE-Rs will need to create the meaning, interactions, organizational adaptability, and resources that will enable the transformation. That's one part – the Roadmap. Figure 8.1 shows the matrix-like nature of how and where all these elements weave together. The *Plan* phase provides the much-needed structure to ensure that (a) CHANGE reaches sufficient depth and breadth across the organization and (b) connectivity and reinforcement are maintained across all content, actions, and activity.

The other part is that the DOWE team needs to also plan for how they will *Manage, Measure,* and *Sustain* the transformation in accordance with the Roadmap – those are the Action Plans. PLAN covers *what* will done and *how* it will be accomplished by developing the Roadmap and the accompanying Action Plans.

Regardless of what is planned, several "truths" about organizational change need to be acknowledged. First, no change happens perfectly, and not every person aligns with the change. However, the better it is, the greater the ROI (LaClair & Rowe, 2002). The aim is to manage change the best way possible, for as many people as possible. Determine "the tipping point" that triggers significant, widespread change and work toward it (Gladwell, 2006).

Second, change is best achieved through commitment, not compliance (Senge et al., 1999. p. 13). To take it one step further, *genuine* change won't happen without people's *genuine* commitment (Hamel & Zanini, 2014). Change must elicit real and authentic meaning. Those involved with the DOWE initiative are presumably committed. Not everyone else is there yet, so the conditions must be set to bring people onto the same page. Their work situation, the one they have grown accustomed to, will be different. For some, buying into change is as big a deal as renegotiating their psychological contract with the company. While change might be for the better, this can still be scary to some. Therefore, manage to the emotional journey (as described in the Change Primer). What needs must be met for a pleasant trip? How will people be equipped to align and move forward?

Third, remember that no plan, strategy, design, progress, or change happens without people. Therefore, remain people-centered – structure all activities to produce desired behaviors and mindsets that lead to extraordinary

Figure 8.1. Roadmap Matrix.

	INDIVIDUAL			TEAM			ORGANIZATION		
	BEFORE	DURING	AFTER	BEFORE	DURING	AFTER	BEFORE	DURING	AFTER
LEARN									
ENGAGE		BUILD MEANING, INTERACTIONS, ADAPTABILITY, AND RESOURCES							
COMMUNICATE									

experiences at work. Don't get caught up in process and tactics or lose sight of why the initiative exists: for people.

As has been the case throughout the DOWE process, the planning and implementation of CHANGE will also be iterative, so be prepared for multiple learning loops.

This phase, PLAN, organizes the content for the Roadmap and Action Plans along with *Manage, Measure,* and *Sustain.* Read chapters 8 and 9 first before moving forward with the DOWE process. Document the DOWE team's progress in one place with the Roadmap and Action Plans document.

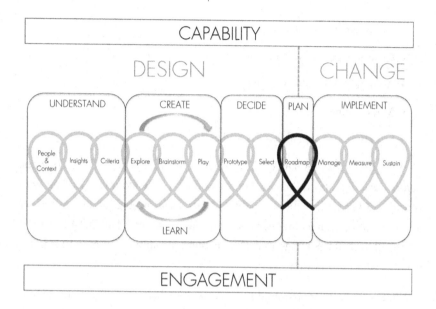

ROADMAP

*REMINDER: The following pages provide guidance and advice for major changes within large organizations. Scale down these activities to the appropriate size of your specific initiative. Also see Chapter 10 for more on how to adapt DOWE at a smaller scale.

Input: DOWE Strategy and Design Blueprint, knowledge from UNDERSTAND, learning from the Change Primer

Output: Roadmap and Action Plans document

Mindset:

- Opportunistic and generative

- Creative and practical

- Strategic thinking and organization

- Decisional

<u>Behaviors:</u>

- Apply what you've learned

- Generate ideas collaboratively

- Assume different perspectives

- Make connections

- Structure and organize ideas and actions

With *Roadmap*, the DOWE team first establishes *what* needs to be done *before* deciding *who* does it or *how* it's done. This encourages leading with strategy rather than tactics or politics. Start with the big picture and never lose sight of it, even as the focus becomes more tactical. The DOWE team is equipped with the Strategy and Design Blueprint and some initial ideas for rollout. Now they must answer:

- What conditions are required for successful realization of the design? How will those conditions be established?

- How will the organization and its people react to the change(s)? What barriers or resistance must be addressed to encourage readiness?

- What can be mined from user research or insights to inform about perceptions and motivations for change?

- What capabilities do people need for this change? Which strengths should be utilized and what should be developed?

If any of these questions are unclear or only partially clear at this point, the team should pause to discuss and engage with users before planning and implementation, if necessary. Consider conducting user research on a smaller scale (e.g., more users, but less activity or fewer users with greater spread across the organization), this time focusing on change experiences and readiness for change. As needed, circle back to pilot or prototype again, but in different ways. In DESIGN, the team assessed the viability and the functionality of ideas and concepts in *Prototype*. For CHANGE, these interactions should provide quick learning on people's reactions to the selected design(s) and how the ideas might scale.

Another option is to host a full-scale Appreciative Inquiry Summit. Much has been written on the benefits of bringing together the "whole" to build and understand readiness for change and co-design the future. Get as many stakeholders as possible into one place to share the DOWE design, gauge responses, interact, and collaborate on initial rollout plans. Having everyone there means that there's access to all the knowledge and talent in the room so planning can be more complete. The need for this was never more evident than in a workshop I attended. When it came to planning changes for an organization's process, no one person knew the existing process in its entirety – only their specific parts in it – and not everyone was there. Because of that, planning was so much more theoretical and incomplete. See *Appendix G* for an example of a modified AI Summit Agenda. The materials produced from the summit speeds up the DOWE team's planning iterations as they organize activities and tasks for the *Roadmap* loop. These options might feel like a lot of additional work, but they pale in comparison to the consequences of change done poorly and the efforts required for fixing it.

How to PLAN

Planning works best if it starts with the big picture and works its way into the details. Reversing this order makes it more difficult to tie individual tasks to the greater purpose. Therefore, PLAN is structured as a series of iterative and progressive exercises to incorporate the Strategy and Design Blueprint, consider different vantage points, generate ideas, and organize change work. The products of these efforts, the Roadmap and Action Plans, guide the remainder of the DOWE process through IMPLEMENT. Each of the following planning rounds are structured to help the team to focus on the task at hand as they develop the Roadmap. Some will move quickly. Others, particularly Planning Rounds 4–7, will require more time and effort.

Round 1: Merlin Exercise

The Merlin Exercise is a good way to see the biggest change components first, starting from the end and building backwards. Used for many years by billion-dollar companies, it's a collaborative exercise that creates alignment through discussion (Fulmer & Perret, 1993, p. 47). Attention shifts from the present to the future, utilizing a "unique blend of creative intuition with rigorous analysis" (Fulmer & Perret, 1993, p. 51). Here's the step-by-step:

1. Start with the outcome: the implementation of the Strategy and Design Blueprint.

2. Determine the major milestones that indicate progress toward that end, beginning with the farthest point and backing up. Describe the milestones with characteristics or conditions that indicate achievement.

3. Discuss and alter sequencing as necessary, ending with the present state and the first milestone.

4. Add framing around time – how long will the entire journey take? How much time will each unique milestone require? Be realistic with expectations, for change takes time. Capture the results of the exercise in the Roadmap and Action Plans document.

Round 2: Maturity Model

In this round, reverse direction and envision growth *toward* the outcome. Maturity models come in many shapes and forms, but the general idea is to take the milestones (from Round 1), line them up, and map out the stages as the organization evolves toward being ready and capable of that future state. Most maturity models have anywhere from three up to 10 stages of maturity, but having five stages is usually sufficient and applicable to most situations. For each stage of maturity, develop a description, determine what needs to happen, and identify the capabilities needed to support each progressive level. Discuss the pace of change needed to achieve each maturity level. How does that timeframe correspond to the timing from the Merlin Exercise, or is it different now? The comparison can be used to validate the team's estimates and provoke further dialogue. There are many examples of maturity models online, but try to create a first draft that reflects your unique initiative without outside influence. Then compare it against what's out there. Tweak as necessary, but *stay true to your organization's specific context and purpose*. Then update the Roadmap and Action Plans document with the maturity model.

Round 3: Burke–Litwin Model

The Change Primer in *Appendix F* introduces and explains the Burke–Litwin Model in greater detail. To summarize (Figure 8.2), this visual can be used to understand and plan for the impact of change across the organization's system.

Each box and block arrow can be viewed as possible "levers" for the team to examine and "pull" as necessary for CHANGE. Using the results of Rounds 1 and 2, determine where change needs to happen in the system.

Figure 8.2. Burke–Litwin Model.

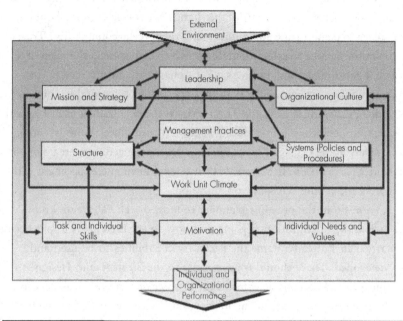

Which levers will be impacted by the change, and how? In what order? Discuss which areas are most ready for change and identify where more work is needed to build readiness. Document this discussion in the Roadmap and Action Plans and combine it with the content in *Round* 4.

Round 4, Part A: Roadmap Ideas

The bulk of the Roadmap is developed in this round, so allocate sufficient time to be creative and have fun with the co-creation. Think of new and different ways to deliver change with impact. Here are some prompts and tips on what to plan for learning, engagement, and communication at the organization, team, and individual levels:

- *Organization:* When planning for the organization level, the mindset shouldn't be about forcing or willing change to happen, but instead should move "from sold to invited" on a massive scale (Hamel & Zanini, 2014). Whether the employee or their employer does it, a choice will be made at some point as to whether a person evolves with the organization. Revisit expectations of employees in the original DOWE Agreement (Chapter 4).

Think about the universal behaviors needed across the organization to successfully change toward the Blueprint and how to elicit them. Once employees decide to be a part of the change, what mechanisms should be in place to demonstrate commitment and reinforce accountability? True commitment begets real accountability, which can come in the form of actual performance and business goals, behaviors, and enforced norms. Don't confuse accountability with the expected (and acceptable) mistakes made in the spirit of learning. This is critical for maintaining psychological safety for people, especially during change. (Learn more about psychological safety in the Change Primer.) Ensure the change activities create opportunities for people to demonstrate their commitment and experiment with success and failure across the organization.

- *Learn*: From the previous planning rounds, the DOWE team knows where the organization is going and how to get there. If it hasn't been articulated already, name the necessary capabilities to be used and developed. These should trace directly to the Strategy and Design Blueprint. Also consult with executive sponsors and other leaders to validate the most urgent capability needs. Select or articulate the behaviors that demonstrate those capabilities. Competency libraries such as Lominger (from Korn-Ferry) provide validated frameworks, descriptions, and terminology to share. Perhaps your organization already established a competency framework that *works effectively*. If so, use it. It's unnecessary to reinvent the wheel unless the one you have doesn't fit the organization's future context.

    Connect the list of capabilities and behaviors with the organization's existing Learning and Development infrastructure, if there is one. Whatever learning interactions are planned, make sure they are purposeful, with identified learning objectives tied to meaningful experiences that consistently support and practice developmental growth. Learning through experience happens by repetition and exposure (Garvin, 2000, p. 93), which means practice and immersion should be part of the plans.

- *Engage:* Robust planning is required to make a difference when it comes to employee engagement. Corresponding actions must cultivate meaningfulness, credibility, and trust. Planning engagement on an organizational scale requires setting up the structure, establishing expectations, and creating opportunities where people can experience the change and interact with it. Create a journey map of the desired change experience, describing the attraction, entry, engagement, exit, and extension (Kumar, 2013, p. 179). Use learning to facilitate engagement, where "'you cannot change how someone thinks,' but you can give them a tool; 'the use of which leads them to think differently,'" as Peter Senge writes (Senge, 2006, p. 286). Engagement should provide guidance and support throughout the emotional journey, with the ultimate goal to increase overall employee engagement with the organization and on the job (Saks, 2006, p. 615). Also plan for:

- building engagement through many resources, made available on a broad basis. (Learn more about resources and why they are important in the Change Primer.) Create a number of touchpoints for employees that encourage psychological safety, adaptability, and openness to change, as well as the adoption of changes – all practiced in safe environments.

- engagement as a feedback mechanism in forums or platforms where information can be continuously exchanged between employees and the organization.

- engagement that exposes and usurps organizational resistance points and barriers that contradict the Blueprint's intent, such as organizational structures, norms, or practices and people's misperceptions or mindsets.

- appropriate expectations of timing and pace that are realistic but also drive change and engagement. The emotional journey often begins with a honeymoon phase, where the novelty of the initiative is exciting and the new has not yet conflicted with the old. This is a critical point for engagement activities: capitalize upon the optimism and set people on the desired path in the emotional journey of change. Be purposeful in creating many touchpoints and put them at key moments of the journey.

• *Communicate*: Communication is both a key component and tool in successful change management. As change disrupts the status quo, people also have greater needs for communication. Communicating strategically, with impact, and in concert with all aspects of the change doesn't happen without thoughtful planning. Develop a communication plan to align with content for Learn and Engage. Messages must be clear,

succinct, and powerful. Information overload can dilute the message, so
be sure that recipients know what is most important and what needs
their understanding, focus, and attention (Senge, 2006, p. 125).
Establish key messages and distribution channels for communication. It
is here that the new narrative for the organization is created and shared,
and shared, and shared, over and over again, encouraging people to
change or adapt their behaviors (Brown, 2009, p. 105).

The power of a well-told story cannot be underestimated. To witness
this first-hand, watch an Irish storytelling competition online or in
person and pick out what makes the stories moving, memorable, and
convincing.

Tom Kelley of IDEO highlighted seven reasons to tell stories:

Storytelling builds credibility.

Storytelling unleashes powerful emotions and helps teams bond.

Stories give "permission" to explore controversial or
uncomfortable topics.

Storytelling sways a group's point of view.

Storytelling creates heroes.

Storytelling gives you a vocabulary of change.

Good stories help make order out of chaos.

(Kelley, 2005, pp. 254–257)

For the DOWE initiative, decide how the new narrative will be heard,
embodied, and realized. How might people of the organization co-create
the narrative?

As a resource, communication helps people to know what the change
means and how it impacts them, what the expectations are going forward, and how they can find support. This content should be informed
by the in-depth knowledge that was acquired through user research.
When questions are anticipated and answers provided ahead of time, the
organization demonstrates its preparedness and concern for its people.
As a starting point, here are some key message prompts that can be
customized for any variety of DOWE initiative:

— This is a departure from the past, rooted in the present, but future-focused

— The initiative itself and the Strategy and Design Blueprint it produced was created with the people, by the people

— Here is the story of our journey

— The initiative demonstrates the organization's commitment to the journey ahead and to its people

— Here are key steps/milestones/signs of progress for people to look forward to as evidence of real change happening

Branding is a cultural artifact that contributes to the change platform and provides common terminology and consistency. Communication planning for change is not unlike an advertising and marketing campaign. Spread key phrases and images that people can associate with the initiative and share with each other in short hand. As cultural anthropologist and author Grant McCracken writes, "Some cultural shifts are heralded by tiny shifts in language, the disappearance of some terms, and the rise of new phrases" (McCracken, 2009, p. 103). Other best practices from marketing include:

— Key facets for marketing success: (1) Motivation and needs, (2) Positioning, and (3) Segmentation (Briggs & Stuart, 2006, pp. 87–88). Through user research and other interactions with the employee base, the DOWE team should have an understanding of people's motivations and needs and therefore can tailor messages accordingly. Positioning has to do with sharing and having people accept the framing. Recall the profound "a-ha!" moment(s) that came with reframe during UNDERSTAND. How might that effect be re-created for employees on a large scale? Segmentation speaks to the various typographies in a target audience. If the DOWE team developed personas, they can use these to develop communication for various segments of the employee population.

— The success of sales is not determined by ad awareness but by the meaning of the brand to its consumers (Briggs & Stuart, 2006, p. 127). The implication for DOWE is that it's not enough for people to be aware of the initiative in a passive sense. All messages related to the DOWE initiative must be meaningful and should shape employee perceptions to the degree that they see themselves as involved and part of the change.

– Surround sound marketing works like a stereo system, so that "each message plays the role of one of the speakers...By working together, each one doing something slightly different, but all working together in concert, the totality of the system creates a more powerful experience for consumers and the marketer achieves better results" (Briggs & Stuart, 2006, p. 155). Every touchpoint where employees encounter the DOWE initiative, including on the job, should reinforce integrated key messages repeatedly in surround sound (Briggs & Stuart, 2006, p. 149).

Learning, engagement, and communication activities across the organization should provide numerous opportunities for people to align with the change. Delivered with quality and consistency over time, they will help to bring along those that need more time.

Team: While organization-level activities provide structure and consistency, change experienced in the team setting is closer to people's day-to-day lives. The change that comes with DOWE is an opportunity to not only strengthen teams in general, but to experiment and practice with new capabilities, behaviors, and experiences.

As DOWE-Rs experienced first hand, the team is where the talents and actions of an individual are amplified. J. Richard Hackman, noted organizational psychologist at Harvard Business School, identified five "enabling conditions" especially needed by teams throughout change:

1. Clear boundaries of membership with work that requires interdependency among team members

2. A compelling purpose that makes a difference for people

3. Good structure that balances size and mix of skills with healthy norms

4. An organizational context that supports the team's success with resources and information, performance, and reward systems.

5. Access to valuable coaching for the team as a whole and its members (Higgins, Weiner, & Young, 2012, p. 370).

Team activities and resources for Learn, Engage, and Communicate should be designed to create these enabling conditions, not just on an event-driven basis but as an ongoing state before, during and after CHANGE. The work of each team should also tie back to the change and the overall business strategy, so that everyone understands what is being achieved as an organization and where their particular team contributes to it.

- *Learn*: Plan resources and learning opportunities for teams to learn, practice, and work together toward the change. Performance and development goals at the team level should call for a high degree of interdependence, where members have to work together to accomplish their goals. Individual efforts and accountability can and should coexist with the collective benefits of team cohesion and motivation. New activities may be introduced as part of the change. Have teams weave these into current or ongoing work.

  Formal and informal team leaders should model and support learning and innovation on the team by structuring work and its conditions to elicit ingenuity and experimentation. This can entail use of tools that increase and develop creativity of ideas, allocation of time to develop new concepts, facilitation of experimentation and learning, and encouragement of innovation in both words and actions (Yukl, 2009, p. 51).

- *Engage*: As the Blueprint is implemented, teams interact within themselves and with other teams to find meaning in the change(s) and understand their role within it. Engagement at the team level should provide tools that empower a self-review of team dynamics, foster team identity, and strengthen cohesion while enhancing diversity. This includes the team-building work to support change readiness in groups. Psychological safety must be addressed and maintained. The DOWE team also designates certain activities and achievements to be accomplished as a group.

- *Communicate*: Communication at the team level brokers the information flow between individuals and the greater organization. Much of the work for Engage and Learn necessitates plentiful use of communication. In addition, the information distributed across the organization is translated and applied, team by team. These are opportunities for the team to discuss, ask questions, and provide feedback. In doing so, the team also generates its own knowledge, which builds additional, self-perpetuating resources. Teams often only need the conditions and empowerment to have these interactions.

Individuals: Every individual experiences their own journey with the organizational change. The DOWE team, as the proxy for the organization and its people, provides the experiences, resources, and opportunities to facilitate change — in excess — so that individuals can choose based on preference and need. To understand further why such a degree is needed, review the Change Primer in Appendix F.

- *Learn*: Once it's understood that the organizational change and implementation of the new design is a learning opportunity, the goal is to equip individuals to build and use their capabilities in ways that support the cause, such as new ways of working, different behaviors, and opportunities to practice and apply knowledge. Begin with helping people increase self-awareness, especially of how they learn best. Honey and Mumford published an easy learning style assessment with accompanying materials, one of many useful tools available. Guidance on which capabilities to develop is generated at the organization level, and this becomes the starting point for individuals to decide, with help from their managers, how to personalize their development.

  Learning opportunities should be plentiful and accommodate for different learning styles and environments. Content should promote adaptability from the very beginning so the employee can deal with upcoming changes (van den Heuvel, Demerouti, Bakker, & Schaufeli, 2013, p. 19). For example, teaching improvisation skills and providing multiple opportunities to practice them on the job creates a greater tolerance for the unknown and a willingness and capability to work with the unexpected. Books like *Improv Wisdom* offer guidance to follow and hone over time (Madson, 2005).

  Practicing new skills, capabilities, and behaviors allows individuals to demonstrate commitment, but this is only possible if they understand their part in the change and how it ties to the organization as a whole. Create situations where people can ask questions and experiment with new skills and behaviors in a psychologically safe setting. Set conditions that enable them to seek and acquire information and thus make sense of the organizational change. This can be further supported by providing resources that engender positive feelings like confidence and optimism (Shin, Taylor, & Seo, 2012, p. 730).

• *Engage*: Engagement is a two-way street. It's a feedback mechanism that creates greater understanding and reinforces the ties between individuals and the organization. As is the case in design, engagement is about creating a rich experience where people can participate and, in doing so, become more committed.

Create a journey map of how the DOWE-Rs want people to experience the change and the Strategy and Design Blueprint. Then plan for multiple, ongoing interactions aimed at increasing individual engagement throughout the change, both in and outside of learning activities. Every individual should have exposure to the degree they can sense and feel the change while it's happening. Without this kind of connection, you are asking people to simply have blind faith, which is an unrealistic expectation on a large scale over a period of time. Progress has to be seen, felt, and shared in real time.

• *Communicate*: Make multiple communication channels available to everyone without causing information and change overload. People should have a choice of where they can acquire accurate information, make meaning, and provide feedback. The first line of communication often happens for individuals through their own network, beginning with their manager and immediate coworkers. These, however, shouldn't be their only resources. The more inputs they have access to, the better they can make their own informed opinions. If there is any confusion, they'll know where to go for help.

Round 4, Part B: Organizing Content

Each planning round thus far generated a diversity of ideas and thoughtful consideration for planning. Determine which meaningful ideas, resources, and actions would best drive change toward the new experience. How will recognition and accountability be planned for each anticipated change? What offerings will be available to employees based on their needs or vantage point? How will new hires be introduced once change begins?

Organize your plans into the Roadmap matrix in Figure 8.3 below, completing one table per each stage of maturity. This format helps the team (1) determine if there's sufficient content to fuel momentum for change and (2) makes certain that each stage of maturity is established well enough to

Figure 8.3. Roadmap Matrix.

	INDIVIDUAL			TEAM			ORGANIZATION		
	BEFORE	DURING	AFTER	BEFORE	DURING	AFTER	BEFORE	DURING	AFTER
LEARN									
ENGAGE									
COMMUNICATE									

advance toward the next. Once drafted, review your table(s) in its entirety and address any shortcomings. Do activities provide consistency with variety before, during, and after change? (Before, During, and After correspond with key change actions – unfreezing, moving, and freezing – see the Change Primer.) Where are the connection points that support alignment and reinforcement?

Also remember to plan the approach for periods of stabilization, where there is a purposeful lull in activity to allow for change to take hold and for people to get used to new environments. In Figure 8.3, the "after" column represents these plateaus. They also exist in between maturity levels. Actions during plateau periods should relieve tension in the organization and offer an opportunity for people to slow down and reflect; they are not to be misinterpreted as periods where nothing happens. What can be planned to rejuvenate resources (psychological and otherwise) and avoid change fatigue?

Some aspects of the plan will require additional work; they are part of the concerted effort an organization makes to purposefully create the conditions of their new work environment. For everything else, make an attempt to dovetail and integrate the change as much as possible into daily work routines (how work gets done) and the existing infrastructure (such as current processes and programs).

Integration supports the long-term adoption of change as it creates a dense network of connections. The more tightly knit the integration, the more reinforcement an organization has for the direction it wants to go as

Figure 8.4. Integration of Maturity Levels.

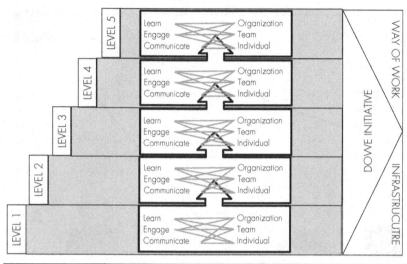

depicted in Figure 8.4. The completed tables, in effect, become the content of your Change Program for the Strategy and Design Blueprint. Add these to the Roadmap and Action Plans document.

Round 5: Visualizing the Roadmap
Next, further refine the plans by developing a visual version of the roadmap. The graphic will communicate the big picture, summarize the buckets of activities (or work streams) in one place, and determine pacing. In effect, this visual bridges the big picture and the work to be done. It can take many shapes and forms – two are given in Figures 8.5 and 8.6 for inspiration and illustration.

The Line of Sight document (Figure 8.5), inspired by other versions in use over the years, is used to indicate short-, mid-, and long-term plans. It emphasizes momentum and sustainability (short-, mid-, long-term), but it can also be revised to align with Before, During, and After. "Feature" could indicate work stream or the DOWE initiative's subtopic/theme or program-matic areas.

Figure 8.6 is another example also inspired by other versions out there. It provides a holistic view of the work streams and their associated activities, color coded to different activities/phases of the change. The best features of

Figure 8.5. Line of Sight.

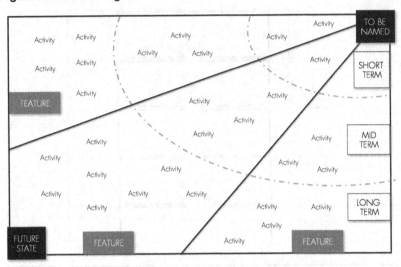

Figure 8.6. Work Streams.

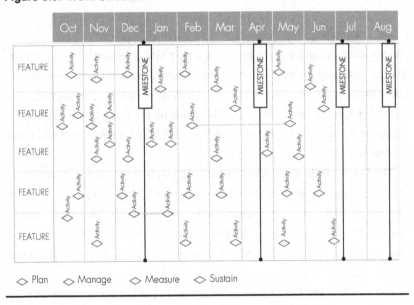

this format are that the team can visualize progress, schedule activities that integrate or overlap, and avoid conflicts or overload. Tip: a roll of butcher paper is a great medium for your first draft.

Both examples are adapted from strategic planning tools that may be familiar to some. Other formats are also encouraged – just make sure they reflect before, during, and after change, work streams, milestones, and sequence. Milestones are important because they give people something to look forward to in the shorter term, indicate progress, and allow achievements to be reinforced and celebrated. The order in which things happen makes a difference, much in the same way authors logically organize and share their ideas in writing. An executive I worked with once said, "First things first, second things second." It may seem like a given, but so many organizations today fail to execute change with the right pacing and sequence. Double check that the activities push progress on an ongoing basis, but be careful to avoid "ritualizing" the change experience by reducing it to a rigid schedule (Harris & Ogbonna, 2002, pp. 37–38). What people should perceive isn't a routine, but rather a characteristically consistent set of affirmative conditions. Add this visual to the Roadmap and Action Plans document.

Round 6: Action Plans for Roadmap
Now that the Strategy and Design Blueprint has a Roadmap, follow up with an Action Plan that details tasks, ownership, and responsibilities for the implementation of the content and related programs. This prevents misinterpretation or misalignment of what needs to be done. Determine what roles and responsibilities are needed across all levels of the organization, based on subject matter expertise, unique perspectives, vantage points, capabilities, and roles. Consider adding resources or perspective from areas such as learning, engagement, and communication functions within the organization, if they exist. The team may also look outside the organization to carefully selected experts or consultants. Their input can be provided for the team's consideration and/or they can help in the implementation of change.

Consider the role Early Adopters (EA'rs, pronounced "ears") could play in the Action Plans for IMPLEMENT. They are the change agents, advocates, influencers, and role models of the organization who evangelize on behalf of the initiative, known to make a substantial difference in change efforts (Battilana & Casciaro, 2012, p. 384) as key resources and sounding boards for employees and the DOWE team alike. For them to serve this purpose, they must always engender trust. Recruit from the employees consulted as part of DESIGN, volunteers within the organization who have since developed interest in the work, or among the strongest connectors whose networks are best suited for the change. The best EA'rs are natural connectors who cultivate large, open networks (as opposed to closed or exclusive). Having too many EA'rs is never a problem, as long as they remain aligned and consistent with the DOWE initiative in their words and actions.

Define the roles and responsibilities executive sponsors, employees, DOWE team members, and EA'rs play and where. This is also an opportunity to fulfill commitments toward the initiative with defined action. Use project management skills to assign responsibilities, articulate needs, budget, track completion, and so on. There are many tools and technologies available that can organize the tasks, minimize or eliminate e-mails, share information, and enable collaboration. There is also the option of going analog — if the workspace has enough walls and sticky notes, go for it. Choose whatever works best for the DOWE team.

Round 7: Action Plans for Manage, Measure, and Sustain

Next, further build Action Plans to anticipate for *Manage*, *Measure*, and *Sustain*. Chances are the team already has some of the answers by this point, but this round is here to ensure adequate preparation. How will plans be managed in implementation? How will change be measured and sustained? Look ahead and review Chapter 9 first, and then come back to answer these questions. There needs to be a mechanism to track the many tasks and decisions during implementation. Figure 8.7 is an example of one template that incorporates the RACI decision model with who is Responsible, who Approves, who's Consulted, and who's Informed.

Round 8: Unintended Benefits and Consequences

Finally, review the Roadmap and Action Plans to anticipate and address unintended benefits and consequences. Establish the response to unintended benefits when they arise so that they can be leveraged for maximum value. How will the team find out about them? How will they be shared with others and made repeatable?

When it comes to unintended consequences, there's always the risk that people commandeer the change to fit their own needs, misinterpret the

Figure 8.7. Action Plan Template with RACI.

	START DATE	DUE DATE	RESPONSIBLE	ACCOUNTABLE	CONSULTED	INFORMED	RESOURCES NEEDED	STATUS	NOTES
GOAL/JOB/OUTCOME:									
Task (in sequence order if possible)									
Task									
Task									
Task									
GOAL/JOB/OUTCOME:									
Task (in sequence order if possible)									
Task									
Task									
Task									
GOAL/JOB/OUTCOME:									
Task (in sequence order if possible)									
Task									
Task									
Task									
GOAL/JOB/OUTCOME:									
Task (in sequence order if possible)									
Task									
Task									
Task									

changes, surprisingly reject or embrace changes, or behave in unexpected ways (Burke, 2008, pp. 265–266). How will the DOWE team address them?

Figure 8.8 starts the discussion and aids with planning. To uncover possible unintended benefits and consequences, consider how *else* people might perceive things as they are rolled out. Look to the extreme ends of interpretation (negative and positive) and fill out what's in-between. Check in with extreme users identified during user research to validate thinking. Color the circles beneath to assess risk level (red, yellow, green) or replace with emoticons to indicate emotions or reactions. This tool highlights the highest risks and opportunities, all in one place. Those identified in the middle are more important and urgent (to borrow terminology from Stephen Covey). Loop back and revise if necessary. Again, there's only so much that can be foreseen, but this last checkpoint prepares the DOWE team as much as possible.

Figure 8.8. POV Range.

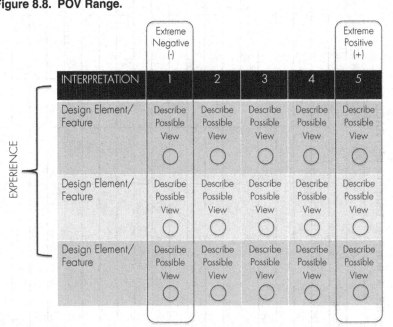

Successful Planning

How is the PLAN phase successful? Start with the desired outcome. This is defined differently by each DOWE initiative, but what they should all have in common is this: a repeatable overall experience that delivers with consistency and reliability (Brown, 2009, p. 124).

Anticipating the natural human tendency to normalize, ask: "Are we as excited for these plans as we were for the Strategy and Design Blueprint? Will these changes remarkably improve work experiences to the degree that it's worth the effort?" If the answer to these questions is yes, then the DOWE team can move forward.

EXPERIENCING PLAN

As a common business skill, the act of planning may be most familiar for DOWE-Rs. It is structured and definitive in ways other parts of the DOWE process are not. Be mindful that despite this comfort level, the team should approach PLAN with continued purpose and meaning that aims to instill inspiration in the organization. Shortcutting or rushing through this process would likewise impact the initiative as a whole. Remember that DOWE's CHANGE is intended to be different (read: better) than all previous change efforts.

There is only so much the team can realistically foresee prior to *Manage*, *Measure*, and *Sustain*. Make the effort to plan as far out as possible with the understanding that things may need to be revisited for ongoing relevance and impact as the organization progresses through each maturity level.

CHAPTER 9

IMPLEMENT

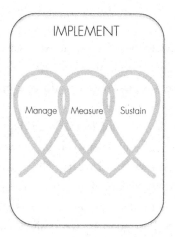

IMPLEMENT OVERVIEW

Everything up to this point in the process was largely achieved as a team. However, IMPLEMENT requires a division of labor, the involvement of more people, and the use of tactical skills to execute Action Plans. This shift has a tangible impact on the DOWE team's dynamics. Deliberate efforts are required to maintain awareness, alignment, communication, and cohesion during this critical phase.

A marked difference in the role executive sponsors play occurs as well (if they were not a part of the core design team). Their support now ramps up to prominent, active involvement as facilitators of CHANGE in partnership with the DOWE-Rs. Employees will seek cues as their leaders recruit and enroll their peers, engage their people, consistently communicate, and model new behaviors. The Action Plans may also designate specific executives based on a combination of what is needed and when, along with individual strengths and organizational roles.

Managers and informal team leaders also join in as CHANGE moves forward. Add support where capability and/or comfort level fall short. This may come in the form of specialized management training, an additional facilitator that allows a supervisor to participate with their team and learn by observation, or a coach who supports the manager as they fulfill these responsibilities.

Take this time to review the roles explained in Chapter 4, which are still in effect. Expound on the expectations now that there is clarity on *what will be*. See to it that these are incorporated into communication content and change activities.

Everything up until now has led to this moment of truth, where vision, design, thoughtful planning, and hard work are about to be realized. This is both exciting and maybe even a little scary. The privilege and responsibility of creating experiences, changing culture, and affecting lives has never felt more real. Pause to relish this as you prepare to make it happen. In the busyness of it all, it will feel so good to see positive change and innovation come to life within the organization. Celebrate it, fuel it, take care of it.

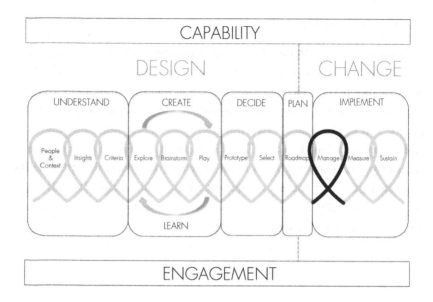

MANAGE

Input: Roadmap and Action Plans

Output: Implemented actions with intended outcomes

Mindset:

- A sense of urgency, organization, and of getting things done

- Optimism

- Evidence-based judgment

- Flexibility

Behaviors:

- Follow through

- Speak up

- Pay attention to what's going on all around

- Collaborate

shouldn't be perceived by others as disengagement. These dynamics at the top have an impact on the rest of the organization, so pay close attention.

Fortunately, this organization recovered from their challenges and the DOWE initiative was deemed successful. Mistakes can be made as long as they are seen as part of the learning process and addressed with corrective action, as they were in this case. In fact, the intervention had a renewing effect on the initiative. They learned from their experimentation and made changes to their approach. Today, they are well on their way toward sustaining their enhanced culture.

Manage is about moving through transitions, rough patches, and unanticipated consequences with agility. By virtue of doing DOWE, characteristics of organizational agility are already incorporated, including alignment, flexibility, openness, innovative thinking, reflection, and learning (Davis, Frechette, & Boswell, 2010, p. 16). Agility is demonstrated by evaluating new information or situations quickly and taking timely, effective actions. I've seen too many after action reviews (AARs) that repeatedly point to the same dysfunctions that a company never resolves. As a result, people may be informed, but they never truly learn. As explained in the Change Primer, learning is defined by *changed behavior*. In the DOWE process, reviews happen throughout the entire initiative to capitalize on positive developments and to make adjustments when necessary, in real time. Change is too important to allow dysfunction to fester, and agility is needed to course correct.

Conscientious planning, executed with agility and managed in the spirit of learning, increases the chances that the Strategy and Design Blueprint will be achieved. Everything else comes down to balance (Senge et al., 1999, p. 61): action with reflection, progress with resistance, stability with instability, flexibility with steadfast purpose. Calibration begins here and continues throughout change execution. Implement the plan, remove barriers, focus on some areas and deemphasize others. Think of it like riding a unicycle, pushing the organization forward, while attempting to stay upright. Remaining purposeful and mindful helps the DOWE initiative strike this delicate balance.

Managing Teams

PLAN supplies the resources needed to empower teams to succeed during change. Set up forums for teams to exchange learning and feedback with each other and to connect with what's going on in the greater organization. Communicate expectations of teams, account for their commitments, track their progress throughout IMPLEMENT, and conduct interventions if needed.

Manage is not just about managing plans and other people, but also managing the DOWE team itself. As previously mentioned, IMPLEMENT requires a division of labor. The DOWE team needs to set aside time and effort to maintain cohesion and open lines of communication when plans are put into effect. Feeding healthy dynamics of the core team is even more of a priority than taking care of other teams in need, for DOWE-Rs must manage IMPLEMENT from a place of strength. If the breakdown begins with the DOWE team, how can the rest of the organization be expected to change? As was the case throughout the DOWE process, schedule and follow through with discussions focused on how well the team is working and how things are going. Reaffirm team norms, make adjustments, confront and resolve challenges, use tools like barometers or pulse checks, communicate early and often.

Managing Individuals

The existence of support mechanisms for individuals throughout the emotional journey promote self-awareness, develop and implement personal development plans, and offer ongoing access to *learn, engage, and communicate resources*. Without them, negative emotional states such as insecurity, fear, or resistance can lead to negative, unacceptable, and/or dysfunctional behaviors that could derail progress. As people interact with one another, make concerted effort to support and spread positivity and resolve negativity. Continuous learning gives individuals skills they need to adapt to new conditions and to address their own conflicts. Accessibility to resources fosters an individual's psychological safety and offers additional help when needed. Members of the DOWE team should avail themselves of these resources as well. A healthy environment is essential for all individuals to thrive through change, beginning with the DOWE-Rs.

If the Strategy and Design Blueprint truly meets business and employee criteria, then most people will choose an experience designed for their success and well-being. At the same time, it's logical to anticipate that not everyone aligns with changes even if they commit to it. Most nonchangers fall into four categories: those that will change only after others go first, those that need more time to change, those that will choose to opt out eventually, and those that actively resist change.

Effective change management should gain enough ground to the degree that nonchange is either neutralized or compelled to respond. Active resisters, especially those who detract from others' experiences at work, should be engaged on an individual basis. Keep in mind that change is about setting conditions that successfully support a new future state. Resist using management mandates or peer pressure to drive people's participation; this undermines the DOWE initiative's honorable intention to respect an employee's right to make choices for their own career. That being said, choices come with consequences, just like cause has effect. People can decide for themselves whether their career aspirations continue to align with the direction of the company. If not, an amicable parting of ways is an option that can happen without hard feelings. For those that remain, DOWE achieves what it set out to do: to get the right people in the right jobs at the right company and to create exemplary work experiences where people thrive.

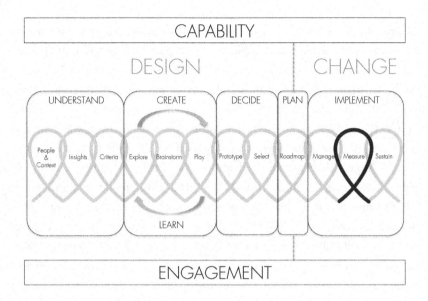

MEASURE

<u>Input:</u> Roadmap and Action Plans

<u>Output:</u> Measurement scorecards/dashboards that provide key change indicators

<u>Mindset:</u>

- Analytical

- Curious

- Solutions- and strengths-focused

<u>Behaviors:</u>

- Apply learning through action

- Look beyond the surface

- Create with strategy in mind

The Measuring Scoop

The role of *Measure* during IMPLEMENT is to gauge progress toward key milestones and enable timely adjustments as part of *Manage*. It keeps the organization honest and self-aware as it needs to be throughout CHANGE. Given its influence, measurements should be strategically determined up front with the expectation that they will change as needed over time. In PLAN, the DOWE team selects the most efficacious metrics, when to use them, and for how long. Some might be used for the entirety of the change process, while others are targeted for specific activities or phases. Point-in-time measurements, which might be event-driven, should integrate with ongoing measurements that track over time to paint a broader, more realistic, and connected picture. Together, the measurements comprise a dynamic scorecard or dashboard that monitors and evaluates the advancement of the DOWE initiative. More than that, *Measure* provides data and content for communication and contributes to the change narrative, transforming hearts and minds, preventing misinterpretation, and addressing gaps between expectation and outcome (Senge et al., p. 285).

DOWE measurements promote change and innovation if they are straightforward, balanced, and meaningful (Keeley et al., 2013, p. 211). For better or worse, people often rely on measurement to enforce accountability. Metrics should therefore be chosen carefully to encourage the right behaviors and discourage the wrong ones. Measurements should never result in dysfunctional behaviors and must be changed if they do. Keep in mind that people can also lose sight of the big picture when there's a hyperfocus on the numbers, so link together all measurements and make them congruent with the overall vision.

Choosing Measurements

Start with measurements for *learn, engage, and communicate* at the individual, team, and organizational levels. Build from there and incorporate them into a dashboard for the entire DOWE initiative. Be sure to also track change management activities, such as responsiveness to barriers and the resolution of unintended benefits and consequences (Harris & Ogbonna, 2002, p. 46). Deliberate on the type of measurements to be used. Qualitative and quantitative measurements each do their job, but come with their own limitations. In the quant versus qual debate, one side argues that qualitative measures aren't tangible enough, while the other says quantitative measures lack meaning or depth. The answer isn't either/or, but rather both.

Having an integrated set of qualitative and quantitative measures enables multiple vantage points on complex challenges such as change (Sale, Lohfeld, & Brazil, 2002, p. 44). According to the experts, there are at least two ways to utilize the combination: by combining two or more to study the same thing or by using one method to enhance another (Sale et al., 2002, p. 48). It should go without saying, but keep in mind all measurements should be captured with people's true permission or consent.

Tips on Quantitative Measures

Quantitative measures capture data numerically and across a large sample size. As previously discussed, many organizations rely so much on quantitative surveys that they ignore other forms of assessment and observation. As a result, they diminish their ability to understand what they really need to know (Senge et al., 1999, p. 284). Use surveys very selectively and only for a portion of the quantitative data. Polls that track 1–2 measures at a time can be a quick and easy substitute. Make sure their frequency doesn't decrease employee response rates. The last thing you want to hear is an employee complaining, "Not another one!"

The DOWE team may piggyback on existing business metrics or scorecards to streamline *Measure*, as long as they are effective to begin with. Don't be shortsighted like the company that fought to preserve survey questions just to have year-over-year comparisons, despite the results being useless. There are other quantitative options as well. Emotion reading technology, such as those used during presidential debates, have algorithms that provide quantitative measures of people's reactions in real time. Social sensing technology uses sensors to track patterns of behavior, providing lots of numerical data.

Examine the impact of all those touch points planned for CHANGE. If the organization has technology in place and a culture that supports transparency, gauge the interactions in frequency, quality, and reach by each person in the organization. Use this to help employees and their managers discuss their personal journey through CHANGE. If, however, the DOWE team prefers information in aggregate to examine trends, collect it anonymously. In addition to frequency trackers and technology-enabled reports, some of the engagement interactions can be designed for or measured in experiential lab settings. If needed, get help from social scientists who understand requirements for scientific methods to ensure rigor.

In the same way biofeedback can serve as indicators for physical well-being, quantitative measures also provide markers for organizational health. Determine which early-detection signals trigger steps to maintain or enhance the state of the organization. All this is done on an ongoing basis, before anything gets worse and blows up or before positive gains go uncelebrated, underutilized, and forgotten.

Tips on Qualitative Measures

Qualitative measures are not unquantifiable. In fact, they can be more definitive than quantitative measures if they are designed to be pass/fail. For example: Do you like it or not? YES or NO. Was it effective or not? YES or NO. Was the experience GOOD or BAD? These are all qualitative questions. Once DOWE-Rs know the answer, they can dig deeper into context, explore possible explanations and root causes, and plan actions accordingly.

Qualitative measures help the DOWE team to understand and share the organizational narrative. (See the Change Primer to learn more about narratives.) As seen previously during user research, storytelling and other descriptive methods can be powerful. Qualitative research methods measure meaning as it evolves throughout change (Sale et al., 2002, p. 45). They capture what it's like to experience and live through the process, at different times and from different vantage points. They answer: How is the designed experience *lived?*

In the midst of change, in-depth qualitative information is needed in at least three areas: environment (as defined in Chapter 1), perception, and behavior. Environment speaks to the effectiveness, quality, and impact of the new conditions. People's perceptions should be explored, for they influence interpretations of their experiences. These include emotional states or reactions, drawn conclusions, and/or "takeaway value" – what they walk away with (Solis, 2013, p. 115). Observe behaviors as reactions to what people learn and perceive. When new behaviors are consistently repeated by more and more people, it becomes a cultural norm that signals change taking hold on a more permanent basis, defining the new way of work. Measure for each of these elements in learn, engage, and communicate activities and on the job. Capture descriptions of the tone, illustrative examples or stories, and/or root causes. Then build insights from them that inform action.

Qualitative measurements are not just for the DOWE team. Individuals can be encouraged to use these tools to reflect on their own experiences in the midst of change, as part of the learning process. Reflection, for example, is a way of paying attention, as previously discussed in Chapter 3. In doing so, people increase self-awareness, solidify learning, and measure their own progress along the journey.

Through change, a new narrative for the organization emerges. The narrative, too, is a qualitative measurement. Storytelling, or the collection and dissemination of stories, spreads the change in ways dispassionate numbers can't. Consider how often people share information by way of stories: what happened, what feels right or wrong, how they reacted, how others should see it, and so on. The narrative that materializes out of change is a huge indicator of how things are going. What stories are being repeated? How are they evolving? How should they be communicated to others? How are people or groups contributing or not contributing to the narrative?

Making Sense (In More Ways than One)

Another thing: whatever's tracked and measured must make sense (Senge et al., 1999, p. 298). All aspects of the dashboard should be aligned and integrated so that they support the success of the DOWE initiative and protect against dangerous misinterpretations. Remember that change takes time, and people sometimes under- or overestimate how long it takes. Just because results don't appear right away doesn't mean that it won't happen at all, and just because it happens quicker than expected doesn't mean that it will stick. Don't let early results declare success or failure prematurely (Senge et al., 1999, p. 287). Treat any large-scale change for what it really is — a long-term business strategy. Change managed consistently over time will reveal how progress compares to expectations, estimates, and plans. Review plans regularly to ascertain whether time estimates are realistic, but remain agile if they need adjustment during implementation.

And finally, never forget that it's never about the metrics themselves, but about people. In DOWE, measurement is not an end but a means, in service of supporting employees and their organization.

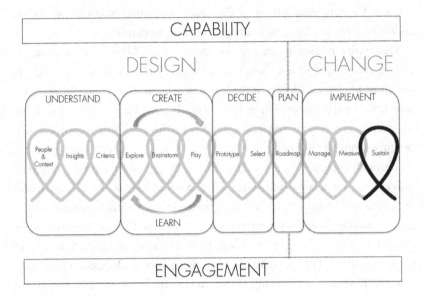

SUSTAIN

Input: Roadmap and Action Plans document and measurements

Output: Sustained change and successful implementation

Mindset:

• Think long term

• Remain self-aware and optimistic

• Be energized

Behaviors:

• Be persistent

• Organize and plan

• Energize others

Why Sustain?

After the excitement of managing change, many organizations fail to follow through with *Sustain*. In some cases, they simply forget to do it. In other situations, momentum slows until activities stop altogether. People might say, "What ever happened to...?" Or worse, "That was a waste. Nothing changed and things aren't any better." It's one thing to move on to the next endeavor purposefully, it's another to just let it happen. Lack of *Sustain* is detrimental to the overall success of any DOWE initiative. For this reason, it is a part of the DOWE process. By this point, the organization has come too far to stop at the doorstep of *Sustain*.

Sustain is defined by how well and how long changes stick for as long as they're needed. This is not a static state, but rather another milestone in an ongoing journey. Both a process and an outcome, the success of *Sustain* is determined by the degree to which momentum for change is cultivated *over time*. As we know from the concept of entropy in physics, what isn't maintained will deteriorate. Organizational entropy occurs when actions and plans aren't sufficient enough to support ongoing change. *Sustain* must make CHANGE strong enough to survive beyond the tenure of its creators if needed, but the length of time really depends on the initiative. For example, an organization might want to sustain changes related to securing a desirable trait longer than a change that is related to a temporary or specific business need.

A variety of circumstances may cause a loss of momentum, such as planning and execution issues, change resistance, politics, poor leadership, lack of effort, or diverted attention. The ultimate test comes down to whether the conditions are in place to support the ongoing existence of the Blueprint once its achieved.

Over a bowl of ramen one day, a former colleague and I discussed why the integration of a business performance methodology didn't last in a company. Millions of dollars and years were spent training this new way of work. The regime changed and from outward appearances the organization seemingly reverted back to its old ways, almost as if nothing happened and people were never exposed to the new thinking in the first place. The real indicator for this was people's behavior. We didn't have the benefit of studying the effect firsthand, but we knew enough to observe three possible culprits. First and foremost, this was a top-down-driven initiative. Projects were designated to use the practice. No real choice, discussion, or change management was incorporated. It simply became the way things are done. Only the people of the organization can tell us whether the transformation happened in their hearts and minds, but they probably weren't asked. Second, the work conditions didn't change in the direction that supported the new way. The company moved forward, and this wasn't incorporated as part of it, at least not overtly. Third, while it may have been a great philosophy and process approach, management of the culture was not part of the equation. What resulted was that the prevailing culture, however it evolved organically, didn't support this way of work in the long term. This story is all-too-common and certainly not unique to this organization. It speaks to how important the conditions and the culture can be when it comes to the achievement of business strategies. You could have the best processes and tools in the world, but success can only be attained through people. More companies should remember this.

There's extensive research on the sustainability of organizational change, an example of which comes from Harvard Business Review. "Why Strategy Execution Unravels – and What to Do About It" names five harmful myths: execution equals alignment, execution means stick to the plan, communication equals understanding, performance culture drives execution, execution should be driven from the top (Sull, Homkes, & Sull, 2015). In stark contrast with these common myths, DOWE strives for (1) continuous alignment, (2) plans that are executed with agility, widespread learning, meaningful engagement and communication, and (3) partnership throughout all levels of the organization. DOWE-Rs are armed with what many other situations don't have: an in-depth understanding of the context, unprecedented engagement with people, and a rigorous process for the design and execution of solutions that create great experiences and cultures.

Sustain actions are woven into the overall DOWE process, particularly in Round 7 of PLAN. If your initiative has chosen to go with a maturity model, sustainability comes built in. The ability to *Sustain* comes down to having enough substance to consistently manage and set the conditions, capitalize on progress, follow through, and navigate away or out of derailers.

Deployment of Sustain

"Getting there" means that the Strategy and Design Blueprint is a reality, an ongoing and consistently lived experience in the organization. *Measure* evaluates the distance to go. *Sustain* calls for paying attention and looping back to *Manage* or even *Roadmap* as needed. The overall sustainability of your DOWE initiative depends on its saturation across the organization, team, and individual levels. Ask: As an organization, has enough been done programmatically and conditionally to foster the change until it becomes "the way things are?" Some organizations can only plan for six months at a time. Change may take longer. If needed, facilitate additional rounds of planning that reflect and build on learning and achievements. Do this especially when there isn't enough robust content and activities planned for *after* the initial implementation. Be sure to also verify the initiative's continued alignment with business strategy.

Secure mechanisms in place for teams to receive ongoing support in their change responsibilities. Measure the extent they are delivering against their interdependent goals, how they continue to nourish desirable team dynamics, the quality and frequency of touch points within and between teams, and their continued alignment with the greater initiative.

Check in with individuals on their emotional journey. How have their perceptions evolved? Do they remain committed, and have they been held accountable to their commitments? If necessary, reaffirm them. Then provide pathways for two-way feedback, ongoing development, and accountability including performance goals. Add resources as needed at all levels to further advance the change agenda.

Be aware that looping back sometimes revisits past anxieties. This was the case with an organization that was one year into its initiative when it had to revisit *Roadmap* in order to *Sustain*. New user research, as a form of measurement, revealed wonderful gains in their culture initiative, but also pointed out where additional work was needed. Despite having already experienced the planning process, people once again felt overwhelmed, much as they had the first time around when so much was unknown. Acknowledging the fears was the first step. People were reminded that they were empowered to set the pace for the new plan's implementation. At the next touch point (a couple of weeks later), anxieties calmed and the initiative was re-energized.

Feed *Sustain* with new information and additional meaningful interactions. What occurs here contributes to the overall narrative as well. As individuals and teams make meaning, they reinterpret the narrative, add to it, discover unrealized connections, and share with others. In doing so, they create continuity in the organizational narrative, connecting past, present, and future (Bartel & Garud, 2009, p. 115).

If the DOWE team is ever stuck or doesn't know what to do for *Sustain*, here are some actions to boost momentum:

- Learn from successfully sustained changes of the past. What conditions were set to create sustainability? What's different this time? What might be worth revising or repeating?

- Reframe and reorient the DOWE initiative with the business strategy, especially if there are modifications in the latter. Define and engage with employees on how the DOWE initiative enables the success of the business and its people. If this is difficult, either loop back in the DOWE process or start a new DOWE initiative as the next stage of maturity for the organization.

- Re-enroll leadership to set direction, demonstrate, and regularly communicate the importance of the DOWE initiative. Mobilize and send out change agents/champions to engage people across the organization again and again.

- Re-examine the Roadmap and the Action Plans — if there isn't enough content to support progressive growth (or maturity levels) over time, then re-PLAN. Be agile and flexible without falling victim to scope creep.

- Revisit the Culture Study, the purpose established for the DOWE initiative, and the Provocative Proposition. Determine the distance to go and take actions to close the gap.

- Along the same vein, ascertain whether *Measure* provided enough guidance on progress and elicited appropriate behaviors.

- Reshare the narrative and stories of the organizational change journey and invite people to contribute to it. Highlight progress and benefits realized as a result of DOWE, including improvements in people's work life and the achievement of business goals.

- Execute the kind of programming that either re-creates the excitement of the initial DOWE initiative launch/implementation or *reminds* people of it. It can also be helpful to host capstone events that celebrate milestones and invite further dialogue.

- Question whether people were truly held accountable to their commitments. If accountability is lacking, renew and re-contract with people. Make it real this time, or the initiative will never be taken seriously.

- Double check the strength of the DOWE initiative's integration with the organization's recognition, performance management programs, and other people processes. Then adjust as necessary.

You'll know you've made strides when employees make the DOWE initiative their own and take action without the need for prompting. The more this happens, the more change is "self-sustaining" on an organizational level (Senge et al., 1999, p. 41). Make sure these new branches on the DOWE initiative tree are encouraged, integrated, and aligned in spirit and consistency with its purpose and principles. It's nothing short of amazing when a transformation takes a life of its own as people embrace it. Those involved can take pride knowing that they've made a difference and changed the course of organizational life for the better.

EXPERIENCING IMPLEMENT

For some, this phase may seem most familiar to their day job. IMPLEMENT is about getting things done well. Others may feel the pressure of high expectations or overwhelmed with so much going on at the same time. Continue as before by acknowledging and managing the fears, leveraging strengths, and celebrating progress. Remaining self-aware and mindful will help the DOWE-Rs and the initiative build confidence to navigate through everything with grace. From their vantage point, the DOWE-Rs have a view of seeing change toward an outcome that they designed, while it's happening. This is truly something very special.

As the DOWE-Rs experience IMPLEMENT, remember:

- Pay attention
- Never hesitate to ask for help
- Confront the good and the bad
- Communicate
- Remain optimistic, agile, and opportunistic.

CHAPTER 10

FINDING YOUR INITIATIVE

Topics covered in this chapter:

- Pilot or miniaturize DOWE

- Challenges

- Applications for DOWE

- When to DOWE

- Benefits of DOWE

- Why you?

The e-mail from my client started with, "Have to share this with you." I worked with this organization to build a culture strategy to reflect their organizational values in their way of work. Employee research revealed that there was a gap between the aspirational and the lived culture. As part of this engagement, the staff defined the behaviors that would demonstrate the espoused values. Afterwards, the VP of Finance and Administration worked with the Facilities Manager to print the behaviors out and pin them up in the new employee-designed collaboration space. Here's what happened in my client's words:

"So yesterday a woodworking company was installing the magnetic sliding doors [in the collaboration space]. The doors will have chalkboard paint as well. One side is for the recognition team (the outer door so they can put things up with magnets) and the inner door which can be used for anything inspirational but mostly as a writing surface for the long work table which will arrive next month. After they installed it, I noted they had it the wrong *way around. We figured out the best solution given some things they had done to one door versus the other which prevented them from swapping them. It was a decent solution, but not perfect.*

Anyway, this morning they were in to make the adjustments and I spoke to them. They had a different solution. They had read our behaviors on their way out yesterday and decided that they could do better so put their heads together and figured out a way to do it right. How great is that? Definitely a hi-lite to my day. I'll send a picture tonight."

That the work this organization accomplished reached beyond the employees and positively influenced people outside the company made this story even sweeter. DOWE inspires different behaviors and conditions that have impact, in ways both big and small. They are meaningful because they create ripple effects that spread positive changes throughout an organization. Imagine the fundamental transformation that comes with harnessing and multiplying DOWE-designed conditions.

A WORTHY ENDEAVOR

What are you seeking? Motivation? A worthy project? More importantly, how much are you willing to invest in the engagement of your people? With its many applications, DOWE can have a significant impact on you and your organization. It is not simply a new idea to try out. *It is an inevitability being called out.* Whether they know it or not, many organizations practice elements of DOWE to manage thriving cultures. There's the financial tech company that established an "Experience Team," to "lovingly craft everything that anyone who steps into [their] offices — be it an employee who may stay for a decade, or an investor who may visit for an hour — sees, hears, tastes, touches, or smells" (Zax, 2012). Another organization, a multi-industry powerhouse and disruptor, posted an open position for a "Leader, User Experience Strategic Talent Acquisition" to lead "lifecycle strategic recruiting" that "will focus on understanding the candidate lifecycle and determining creative ways in which [they] can increase touch points with candidates throughout their career paths." Design firms are being hired to create internal people programs for their customers because the branded experience is important, even for employees. A variety of websites showcase employer culture and workspace. They highlight how culture is critical to success and how much people care about it. Some companies regularly publish and distribute their own culture reports to describe who they are, why they're great, and how they plan to evolve.

Chances are, your company also practices some form or aspect of DOWE. Organizational change is managed; learning and development programs grow your talent; employee engagement is measured. Other great practices are in place but perhaps they lack an overarching strategy to weave them together for greater impact in people's lives. DOWE integrates these activities into a cohesive framework that enhances the significance of experiences and the culture at work.

The chances are also good that there are plenty of opportunities for your organization to benefit from DOWE. Perhaps innovation is a corporate value that is yet to be realized because the day-to-day culture doesn't support it. A new and ambitious business strategy may need significant organizational change to be successful. A merger or acquisition has created a culture clash. Your company may need to distinguish itself to attract the very best talent in a tight market. As mentioned before, the possibilities are endless.

Should you choose DOWE, your organizational context will determine how you build a case for it. Make a strong argument for the investment in employee time. The benefits far outweigh the cost in that respect. DOWE requires high engagement, but it need not be expensive or overly complicated. The scope of an initiative determines resource allocation – sufficient dedication of talent and funds supports the conditions for success. Any needs beyond that can be tackled as a design challenge. Take a cue from the guy who was "so tired of how sterile and boring [the] office felt" that he decided to buy over 8,000 sticky notes and recruit his coworkers to create murals depicting pixelated superheroes (Brucker, 2015). The cost of the paper ($300), people's time, and a break in work productivity was nothing in comparison to the long-lasting effects of camaraderie built in the accomplishment of this task.

If your organization truly sees people as a valuable asset, get leadership's commitment and willingness to trust a new process from beginning to end. Begin 1-1 conversations with those you need to support the work. People will be more likely to disclose questions or concerns in a private conversation than they would in a group. If that doesn't work, don't tell them, show them. Demonstrate how people respond when they are engaged. Point out the value of understanding the culture in the way people behave, not just in what they say. Highlight how real change can be when it is generated from within the organization. DOWE is best understood and appreciated when experienced. Use it as the method for the CEO's next think-tank project. Pull together high potential individuals from across the organization to form a pilot DOWE team. Attach DOWE onto another business initiative, like lean implementation, reorganization, change, transition, or an upcoming merger. Use DOWE concepts to create a strategy the company has been thinking about but hasn't gotten around to. Few can say no with a solution in hand to pilot. As you can see, there are many other entry points for deploying DOWE.

A full-blown DOWE initiative can take anywhere from several months up to a year depending on its scope, but an abridged DOWE pilot can be achieved from a matter of days up to a month. Miniaturize DOWE to a small, but important challenge that others care about. Host an Appreciative Inquiry summit that kick-starts or pilots a DOWE initiative. Or rapid proto-type a solution with everyone in the room over a few days (Kelley, 2005, p. 162). Be sure to go through all the learning loops and work collabora-tively. Modify the process to your needs without skipping steps or losing meaning. Engage people through user research, pull profound insights, set criteria, and share the findings. Co-design with others. Once people see the potential in what's created, they will want to keep going. Resist the tempta-tion in this age of "lean" to make pilots your sole approach to DOWE. Culture takes time because people need time. Complexity cannot always be solved for overnight. Once a pilot makes the case for the approach, dedicate the time and the resources needed to fully implement DOWE.

No matter what you do, help people to see the possibilities and the impact DOWE could have for your organization. Impress upon others that different approaches must be taken to get different results. Alternatively, begin DOWE within your own sphere of influence, whether it is with your own team, department, function, or business unit. Or take a really great situation and make it even better with DOWE. Others will take notice. Start small or start big. You'll find that the design of one experience could lead to the design of all experiences. Said one VP after a daylong design workshop, "It makes me think about how much better we can design all these other pro-cesses we attempted to revamp before. We should take this approach from now on." When work experiences are designed and managed in concert with one another, culture can be powerful.

...WITH CHALLENGES

All this being said, practicing DOWE is not without its challenges and vulnerabilities. To the degree possible, this book's intention is to help you and your organization implement DOWE well. There's always the risk of doing "the right thing the wrong way" (Stelter, 2014), however, and there are potential pitfalls along the way. When you combine DESIGN, CHANGE, CAPABILITY and ENGAGEMENT with the unpredictability of people and the volatility of business, things happen.

First, anticipate that difficulty will emerge from time to time. DOWE initiatives are there to address the toughest, most complex challenges faced by organizations, ones that call for taking mitigated risks to achieve meaningful change and innovation (anonymous, personal communication, February 7, 2015). Even when things aren't going well, make the most of these wins, address the root causes, have faith in the process, and remind yourselves that rewarding outcomes are there for the taking if people give it a chance to work.

Keep in mind that DOWE-designed strategies and solutions are never intended to be permanent solutions. Continuous improvement or complete overhauls are necessary for any innovation to maintain relevance. The trick is figuring out when. Use measurements and user research to make informed decisions, long after IMPLEMENT. With DOWE, it's always possible to re-loop back in the process, or even start again from the beginning. When the business context changes, it's an imperative.

Doing DOWE also takes some getting used to. People are accustomed to knowing answers up front, but DOWE seeks to *discover* solutions through its process. The "not knowing" can cause uneasiness in people, even when they understand the intent. As one leader put it, "... it was hard because it was so different than anything else I had done. It's a little nerve-wracking to get your head around managing change when you can't get yourself completely around how it's happening" (anonymous, personal communication, January 9, 2015).

In some environments accustomed to "top-down" initiatives, people are used to guidance that comes from above, so being empowered with co-creation can feel strange at first. Some people momentarily shut down, at a loss for what to do with that empowerment. Insight building, brainstorming, and planning can be especially challenging, even if everyone is capable of learning and accomplishing it — that is, if they are willing.

Others might have a hard time shifting from problem-centered (restrictive) to opportunistic (appreciative) mindsets. Instead of letting "what's wrong" drive actions, DOWE sets the atmosphere for what's right. Some folks can't help but to slip back into problems because that's where they've grown accustomed to working. These and other anxieties must be acknowledged and persistently managed with agreed-upon norms. Focus should remain on the goal or purpose that is driving DOWE. When feeling lost, use the DOWE process like a map to find where you've been, where you are, and where you're going. Once anxieties are addressed, undivided attention can be directed to activities at hand.

In addition, doing DOWE develops and calls upon additional skills that are often underutilized or underdeveloped in business, like strategic perspective, observation, empathy, intuition, creativity, and mindfulness. As said previously, there are periods where strengths shine, but other times where people may feel less assured while building new capabilities. This can be uncomfortable for some. Provide reassurances when needed and encourage people to work through the discomfort. Eventually everyone will find resolution as the DOWE process moves forward.

With or without DOWE, lack of accountability is a common organizational shortcoming that undermines the credibility of any initiative. Not addressing issues on time, or at all, is a fail. Reluctance to hold others, especially leaders, to higher standards can be seen as a lack of commitment on the part of the organization (anonymous, personal communication, January 15, 2015). People will wonder why they should commit when others do not, even when DOWE works in their best interests. This is especially true when it comes to how leaders behave. One glassdoor.com review said, "… leadership claims to be transparent but isn't, culture is heavy-handed and values are not embodied by senior management …" Employees won't adopt a culture if this is what they perceive, no matter how great it sounds. To reiterate, DOWE cannot be successful without commitment and accountability *at all levels*. Get agreement on expectations and hold people to them.

DOWE can also generate really sleek, out-of-the-box ideas, but their value should only be judged based on their meaningful impact and effectiveness — not the coolness factor. Sometimes the most profound innovations are the simplest. Resist the temptation to become mesmerized by novelty's bells and whistles and remember that at its core, DOWE is about helping people thrive at work. Make sure all elements of the designed experience have strategic value and get rid of superficial window dressing.

Last, but certainly not least, the essence of the DOWE concept is free from politics – it seeks truth through the voice of the whole (a combination of the employee and business) and designs from evidence-based conclusions "without fear or favor," as *The New York Times'* slogan proclaims. DOWE observes "what is" like a scientist, brainstorms like a designer, and implements like successful innovators by making it a reality. Nevertheless, DOWE can fall prey to dysfunctional organizational dynamics that influence the direction or the implementation of the initiative. They include resistance to change, biased thinking, personal agendas, infighting, lack of commitment, inconsistency, failure to persist, and the like. So-called organizational snipers may be lying in wait to criticize or slander at a moment's notice. Their attacks can range from minor distractions to public uproars. If permitted, not only will the initiative fall short of its potential, but unwanted cynicism or frustration may result. People might turn their blame on to the concept when the true failure comes from deep flaws within the organization and – quite frankly – in its leadership.

These and other adversities will reveal themselves as long as you're paying attention. What doesn't work will be evident. Address, seek to understand, and neutralize threats. Practice agility to quickly learn and recover from the inevitable stumbles. Reorient and course correct as necessary. Iterate your way out. Amplify the employees' point of view. Show progress. Review and remind others of the provocative proposition. Act according to agreed-upon norms. Challenge the organization to live up to its commitments, honor the spirit of DOWE, and hold people accountable. Feeling stuck can always be treated with a short break or outside perspective. Know that there's always a next step and new possibilities to pursue.

DOWE provides a framework and an environment where challenges are expected, not feared. No one said creating stellar experiences at work would be easy, but again, it's a very worthy cause. Doing DOWE is more than just the end result, it's also about the journey. You, your employees, and the organization will grow and transform together through this shared experience.

WHAT TO DOWE?

By now, this book has equipped you to answer why DOWE exists and how it should be practiced. When to use it and on what may still be a question for you or your organization. There are countless (or more boldly, universal) applications for DOWE. Prime targets exist wherever people are involved, culture is reflected, and experiences are lived. In any given organization, there's a treasure trove of opportunities to pursue. In general, there are at least three possible scenarios as starting points.

Perhaps you have a particular business problem you can't solve or an ongoing or upcoming organizational challenge. In these cases, identify the opportunity space, but let the process do its work. Defining the problem too narrowly up front will unduly influence the output with predefined answers, missing out on game-changing insights and preventing DOWE from reaching its full potential.

On the other hand, an organization may have no idea where to start despite acknowledging that something needs to be done. Never fear. The DOWE process establishes what needs to be designed. UNDERSTAND's *People & Context* and its accompanying Culture Study defines "What Is" and reveals the biggest influencers of the work experience along with their unmet needs, in priority order.

Prime targets for DOWE may also appear in the existing infrastructure or current state of the organization, such as specific business and strategic needs, operational or functional areas, and other fundamentals like those represented on the Burke–Litwin model (Figure 8.2). Consider the forthcoming suggestions as thought starters and sources of inspiration. Start with a look at how DOWE might be applied to broad business strategies and operations (Figure 10.1).

All aspects of the employment life cycle from recruitment through retirement are experiences that can be purposefully designed – policy, process, or transaction. Challenge the organization to go beyond the surface of "getting it done" and design for the *experience* of "what it's like." You might want to design whole strategies or experiences by category (i.e. Recruitment or Talent Management) or consider questions within each category that enable people and the business to be successful.

All types of interactions can be enhanced by DOWE, since they're experiences people encounter at work (Figure 10.2). In-depth exploration of the

Figure 10.1. Business Strategy DOWE Targets.

BUSINESS STRATEGY	HOW MIGHT THE ORGANIZATION...?
Mission and Values	• Define why it exists along with its place in the world? • Align business and people strategies with mission and values? • Establish values that reflect the mission? • Create a work environment that reflects the mission and values? • Instill mission and values in its people and the way of work?
Operations	• Establish governance without bureaucracy? • Make decisions involving the right parties? • Collaborate between business units, functions, departments, and teams? • Continuously improve key business processes by co-design? • Have consistency while empowering people? • Design effective, user-centered business processes? • Make IT, HR, Finance, etc. more user-centered?
Long-term Strategies	• Develop these plans and a matching people strategy? • Evolve the culture with these strategies? • Align stakeholders throughout each stage? • Galvanize the organization around the strategies? • Define progress and set expectations for employees?
Turnaround	• Create excitement around business challenges? • Select the right decision makers and teams for success? • Frame the turnaround as opportunities? • Empower people and assuage fears and distractions in order to make progress? • Identify the true root causes of the challenges and build the case for change?
Growth Plans	• Simultaneously grow the business and the organization's talent with purpose? • Determine and manage the changes that come with growth? • Scale up without losing key aspects of the culture?
New Markets	• Identify and work with partnerships and markets that align with company mission and values? • Acquire in-depth insights of new markets and whether capabilities are in place to support them?
Mergers and Acquisitions	• Culturally assess all organizations involved as part of due diligence? • Co-create a new combined culture? • Acculturate newcomers purposefully? • Manage transitions to be minimally disruptive and make them positive experiences?
Organization Design	• Structure itself for the accomplishment of work? • Remove bottlenecks or barriers in its structure for better business results? • Acclimate people to new structures and ways of work? • Reflect and align with strategy and culture?

Figure 10.2. Employment Cycle DOWE Targets.

EMPLOYMENT LIFE CYCLE	HOW MIGHT THE ORGANIZATION…?
Recruitment	• Align the workforce plan with the business strategy? • Attract and acquire talent that will succeed at the company? • Understand motivations, needs, affinities, and behaviors of targeted talent? • Design for a differentiated candidate experience that embodies the company's culture and selects for fit? • Manage the company's reputation for all candidates, regardless of whether or not they're hired?
Onboarding	• Orient new people, but also get to know them, and make them known? • Help new hires understand the work culture? • Establish internal networks for new hires? • Enable new hires to contribute immediately? • Provide ongoing support past the first few months, first year, and beyond?
Compensation and Benefits	• Create a flexible pay structure that satisfies different needs in talent segments while maintaining consistency and competitiveness? • Present a variety of benefits suited to different lifestyles and life stages affordably? • Align compensation and benefits programs with company values?
Performance Management	• Establish a program that managers and employees find useful for measuring performance and providing feedback? • Make performance management a good use of people's time? • Gauge performance for multi-year objectives? • Set aligned and realistic expectations for performance? • Gather information in real time? • Ensure people know how they are doing at any given moment?
Recognition	• Reward the right behaviors? • Identify multiple avenues through which recognition is delivered? • Make sure recognition is given and received with intended impact? • Recognize individuals without demotivating others? • Reward and incentivize employees in novel ways? • Make recognition last?

Engagement	• Identify and set conditions for employees to increase and sustain their engagement? • Select the best engagement methods for the context? • Determine which business outcomes are directly tied to engagement and leverage for repeatable, positive results? • Strategically communicate to both engage and increase engagement?
Talent Development	• Align personal ambitions with company needs? • Match learning plans with company strategies? • Provide ongoing development that is integrative and progressive? • Weave development with job design? • Define learning experiences for different learning styles?
Transitions	• Purposefully manage going into and coming out of roles? • Transfer knowledge both ways? • Manage people's needs throughout transitions? • Roll out consistently positive transition experiences? • Manage transitions well?
Talent Management, Workforce Planning, and Succession	• Strategically plan for current and future talent needs simultaneously? • Fully appreciate and utilize the breadth of talent within the organization? • Capture, grow, and engage the organization's talent resources? • Align talent management, workforce planning, and succession with talent development and transitions?
Off-Boarding and/or Retirement	• Ensure smooth exits from the organization? • Make the exit experience as positive as the onboarding experience? • Capture institutional knowledge before it leaves the organization? • Re-define the relationship between the employee and the company post-exit? • Consider alternative work arrangements to off-boarding or retirement?

current state and future possibilities sets the stage for change, particularly with long established, but mediocre work practices. DOWE replaces them with innovative new behaviors, mindsets, and tools. Abolishing all e-mail, for instance, can change the way people work, communicate, and collaborate with others. The very idea wouldn't be possible without thoughtful inquiry. Think of other interactions that work, but could do even better with redesign.

Figure 10.3. Interactions DOWE Targets.

INTERACTIONS	HOW MIGHT THE ORGANIZATION...?
Change	• Plan, manage, measure and sustain change successfully? • Identify what needs to be done for learning, engagement, and communication? • Implement change with excellence? • Deal with the impacts of change, both positive and negative?
Coaching and Feedback	• Understand individual needs, motivations, and reactions to feedback? • Have people regularly receive coaching and feedback as positive experiences? • Set expectations and behaviors for good coaching and feedback practices? • Utilize coaching and feedback to manage organizational performance and development?
Collaboration	• Learn about people's experiences with collaboration at work? • Co-design for collaboration that yields business results? • Set the conditions by which people collaborate well? • Design meetings that are effective, efficient, and collaborative?
Conflict	• Promote healthy debate and conflict that results in better business outcomes? • Equip people to manage conflicts? • Balance confrontation and conflict avoidance? • Reset norms when it comes to conflict?
Diversity	• Gain insights from people's perspectives on diversity? • Advance diversity beyond tolerance and representation to harness its advantages? • Set the conditions for diversity to thrive? • Design for positive experiences with diversity?
Leadership	• Define, encourage, and develop leadership behaviors and expectations for the organization? • Develop current and future leadership in support of business goals and strategies?
Management	• Determine the role management plays? • Improve management capabilities? • Make relationships between managers and employees productive?
Team Dynamics	• Equip teams to develop and maintain healthy dynamics? • Make membership on teams valuable experiences? • Get things done through teams?

Workspace	• Explore how people interact with their physical spaces? • Co-design for workspaces that inspire and encourage productivity and engagement? • Secure the design and set up of workspaces to reflect company culture and values?
Work-Life Balance/Conflicts	• Develop and communicate the organization's work-life philosophies in accordance to the values? • Equip every employee for work-life balance according to their own context? • Understand and measure people's experiences around the topic of work-life?

You can also design for a particular organizational capability (i.e. innovation, empathy, or agility), a specific cultural characteristic (i.e. honesty, helpfulness, transparency, or integrity), or a targeted result (i.e. employer brand loyalty, first to market, work–life balance). For these types of DOWE, they can and should be positioned as *learning* initiatives.

How might the organization …?

- Define the capability/characteristic and the behaviors that demonstrate proficiency in it? What must precipitate the outcomes?

- Measure the distance between where you are and where you want to be and define how to get there?

- Leverage capability/characteristic experts within and outside the organization?

- Decide who plays what roles to bring out desired outcomes?

- Put together strategies to realize the capability, characteristic, or result?

- Design for learning?

- Imagine the experience of achieving the vision?

- Weave in the capability or characteristic into ongoing initiatives and the way of work?

- Learn to be an (x, y, z) organization?

WHEN TO DOWE?

A planning session with a client led to a discussion with regard to the timing of "culture work." The president wondered, "When is the best time to do this?" My immediate answer was that there's never a bad time. However, I think the real question was more along the lines of "When is the ideal time to do the work?" A few conversations later, the client mentioned a time a few years back when things were "bad." I asked, "Could that have been a good time to do the work?" They answered, "Yes, I suppose so." It reinforced their decision to move forward, realizing that the timing is always workable.

The "when" question may be asked out of genuine curiosity. For some institutions, culture work is not an everyday happenstance, but rather a big unknown. DOWE makes culture building tangible, actionable, and progressive. The question of when to do the work may also be motivated by concerns regarding money and time. After all, leaders must decide where to invest limited resources. Most people agree that strategic business planning, for its influence on the direction of the organization, is a smart investment. The benefits of developing people strategies are less recognized, despite their ability to support the realization of a company's mission, values, and business goals.

Others may ask "when?" out of fear for what might transpire. In this case, ask what would be so scary about engaging your people on important topics they care about? Is avoidance of confrontation or intervention going to be better or worse for the organization in the long term? Think through the value in truly engaging people in unprecedented ways and bringing forth positive change. Use the Culture Study to determine readiness for change within the organization and then embark on the rest of the DOWE process to align and bring people along.

Then there are those many companies that neglect or refuse to take action until they reach a point of desperation. Even those that speak of valuing their culture and their people may push the work off in favor of other business priorities or because they are simply too busy.

You could wait for the "right time", but there's never really a wrong time to begin engaging people to create new or better experiences in the workplace. How about now?

Because organizational life is a journey and not a destination, there are lots of on-ramps from which to begin the work. Iterating into new business circumstances or new needs is always an option. So while it's understandable that leaders will want to think about when to begin DOWE, the bigger concern is *whether it's done at all*.

Let's consider the different points in time that present opportunities for transformation: at the beginning, in the middle, and at the end. For those fortunate enough to be in start-up mode, there is something special about building a culture from the ground up. Founders often wonder if a small staff is enough to begin culture work. I always respond that if there's a business strategy, then there should be a people and culture strategy to help achieve it. A healthy culture begins with healthy dynamics on the founding team. The best way to avoid founders syndrome (a culture that mimics a founder's personality) is having a people and culture strategy in place from the very beginning to help the business take off. Without it, culture could erode through the course of rapid growth. A CEO could lose the luxury of knowing and influencing everybody directly because there's simply too many people. Subcultures begin to form with or without their knowledge. DOWE helps new businesses manage the scale up purposefully and strategically.

For established businesses or organizations, *the beginning* may be the start of a change or transformation effort, or perhaps the introduction of new leadership. Thoroughly knowing the current state helps you plan for the future. Given that there is actually something to change *from*, it's especially important to understand the culture and engage people up front. Too many companies forget this and pay for it later. People play a major role in change, so make sure they are enabled to help. One executive I worked with abruptly stopped the people initiative already in motion during a major business transformation, despite his prior knowledge and approval. He said he wanted to wait another year into the implementation. The timing was arbitrary, and there was no rationale for why people should not be a priority from day one. Engaging people doesn't distract them, it makes them more focused. Nothing hurts the credibility of change initiatives like inconsistent starts and stops, especially for the 80 volunteers in this case who were motivated and already involved.

Whether you're *in the middle* of business as usual or a big change, DOWE can come into play. Exploring the experience while people are in it gives feedback and insights that can inform actions in real time. This allows you to mindfully tinker in the present and iterate toward a desired future state. DOWE can also be used to instigate course corrections, allowing you to create the roadmap needed to move forward.

The *end*, which refers to the aftermath of a big change, the achievement of goals, or the arrival of a planned future state, all signal a new beginning for most businesses. A different kind of end that comes with closing down a business or unit is also a work experience that can be purposefully designed. DOWE enables organizations in any of these circumstances to establish direction and design for what's next. Managing the new conditions and how people experience them provides consistency and stability by assuaging concerns, identifying fresh opportunities, and setting new conditions to support great work. It operationalizes and reinforces a new social contract between employee and employer. Consider, for example, what happens after a big merger. Do you want people from the legacy organizations duking it out to see which culture wins, or do you want to create a new culture where everyone can work together and create a shared identity?

SEQUITUR

There is a huge range between the best and the worst workplaces. In all likelihood, your organization falls somewhere in between, with some room for improvement and lots of possibilities. In today's era, the "excuse of ignorance" is no longer available (O'Toole, 1995, p. 196). Culture matters. It matters so much that a C-suite executive turns down offers from 17 companies due to fit (anonymous, personal communication, January 27, 2015). It matters so much that a CEO sets out to create a "non-bitchy" company, saying "For me, it's about being straightforward. It's about always knowing where people stand, supporting people, having an environment that really expects great work, but is also a great place to be. Culture is everything. If you have happy people, they do their best work. It's pretty simple" (Rose, 2014).

Every organization has a choice when it comes to the mindful stewardship of its culture and can choose to regard it as a social responsibility. For organizations that don't know how to be any different, but want to be (anonymous, personal communication, January 27, 2015), DOWE provides a way to systematically build culture through experiences. As a result,

Figure 10.4. The DOWE Experience Word Cloud/Wordle.

organizations develop more capability, engagement, collaboration, innovation, relationships, performance, inspiration, success, and so much more.

Figure 10.4 is a wordle of how one leader described what it was like doing DOWE. Though every initiative will be different, what is shared here and throughout this book are some of the hallmark characteristics.

If you are willing to take some of these into your work life, then DOWE is worth a try. What you get in exchange is clarity. Where culture might have been covert, it is made overt. An organization enhanced by DOWE can communicate the most critical requirements of their culture, ensure those they employ share and align where it really counts, and make the most of every other wonderful difference people bring. Now there is a way to determine true cultural fit as a clearly articulated and consistent standard. There's also an opportunity for decisions to be made regarding congruency of potential, new, and established employees – on everyone's part. Knowing the cultural expectations reduces stress and confusion and aligns the organization. The greater the synchronicity between employee and employer, the higher the engagement (Briley & Aaker, 2006, p. 58).

Great culture doesn't have to leave with a great leader. It can be so strong that it outlives its leaders and creates a legacy where future successors have to fit in (rather than the other way around). Values can be so important that a company would walk away from business dealings that don't align with them and still be successful (anonymous, personal communication, January 6, 2015). Culture can attract top talent, offering them a compelling reason to join one company over all others.

Consider the following scenarios: One organization that creates extraordinary experiences at work from a place of strength. Another must redesign their culture in response to serious business challenges. Still another wants to differentiate themselves out of mediocrity and create a true employer branded work experience. And then there's the one that chooses to do nothing. In which context do you find yourself?

Now ask: What happens if *you* don't do something (anonymous, personal communication, January 8, 2015)? People of your organization are already capable of creating extraordinary work experiences; they are prequalified to discover and create what works best. It comes down to choosing the opportunity, having a disciplined framework to guide the way, and following through with it. If there was ever a chance to define meaningful work for yourself and others, this is it. Imagine how different things would be if extraordinary work experiences were the norm. *You* could be the catalyst that transforms the organization. Whatever you choose to DOWE, whenever you choose to do it, all you need to get started is a true commitment to your people, leadership buy-in, a good understanding of the DOWE process, a vision for your desired outcomes, and an amazing DOWE team to lead the way.

DOWE as an acronym was no accident – more than being easy shorthand for Design of Work Experience, it also represents the collaboration required in the Design of WE, as a collective. Now that you've been exposed, there are a number of choices before you. You could wait for others to try it first. You could pick another approach down the road. You could reject this concept altogether or simply ignore it. Or you can give it a go on the possibility that there is an opportunity to tap into the potential within your own workplace. Take these options back to your organization and ask, DO WE?

APPENDIX A: SAMPLE TEAM CHARTER TEMPLATE

TEAM CHARTER TEMPLATE

Our Purpose: Why does this team exist? What is its primary purpose?

Our Process: What process(es) will be developed, implemented, or used by this team? What will guide the progression of activities toward the defined outcome?

Our Norms: • Define behaviors characteristic of this team, its culture and how it will work together (minimum 5–7, no more than 10–12)	Operating Principles: • What principles explain and guide the norms? (minimum 5–7, no more than 10–12)

Source: © Karen Jaw-Madson. www.designofworkexperience.com

APPENDIX B: CULTURE STUDY SAMPLE TABLE OF CONTENTS

1.0 Executive Summary

2.0 Background (Origins of Initiative and DOWE Team)

3.0 Approach and Process

4.0 Purpose and Scope

5.0 Early Assumptions, Key Questions

6.0 Research Methodology and User Research

7.0 Analysis (Business Factors, Major Themes, Minor Themes, Other Factors, and Dynamics)

8.0 Profound/Extreme User Perspectives

9.0 Insights

10.0 Reframe

11.0 Provocative Proposition

12.0 Criteria

13.0 Recommendations

14.0 Next Steps

15.0 Conclusion

16.0 Appendices

APPENDIX C: STRATEGY AND DESIGN BLUEPRINT SAMPLE TABLE OF CONTENTS

1.0 Introduction

2.0 Explore

3.0 Brainstorm

4.0 Play

5.0 Prototype(s)

6.0 Decide (Criteria, Selection)

7.0 Strategy, Design, Intended Outcomes

8.0 Recommendations

9.0 Next Steps (Preview Roadmap and Plan Phase)

APPENDIX D: THE STIMULUS PACKAGE

Approach the problem from a different perspective	Alternate between general (big picture) and specific (detailed) views
Divide the idea or issue into various parts	Reframe the idea or issue
Reorganize the idea or issue from the beginning (start from a clean slate)	Make a wish list for the issue or idea
Change the starting point or work backwards	Frame the issue or idea as a question: "How might we...?"
Look for differences and similarities amongst different concepts or ideas	How do you reframe your idea or issue in an opportunistic, strengths based, or positive way?
Put two polar opposite concepts, issues, or ideas together to create an oxymoron	What is the root cause of the issue? What is that root cause's root cause?
Ask "why?" five times and dig deeper with your answer each time	What rule, policy, or way of thinking has been successful for you, this idea, or this issue in the past but may be limiting now?
Take a break and do an activity that has nothing to do with this issue or idea. Clear your head, and get inspiration from that other activity.	Pose the idea or issue as a "What if?" proposition
Dig deeper. Don't stop with the first right answer you find. What are the 2nd, 3rd, or 4th right answers?	What assumptions are you making? Which unnecessary assumptions can you eliminate?
What patterns do you detect? How can you use them to understand your idea or see it differently?	What other senses can you use to develop your idea or solve your issue? (Sight, sound, feel/touch, etc.)

What other things does your idea or issue remind you of? What associations can you use to develop the idea or issue?	What would a six year old see or say if they were considering your idea or issue?
What rules can be challenged in this idea or issue and what new approaches can be freed?	What whacky things can you do with your idea or issue?
What can you edit out or constrain to make the idea or issue better, more streamlined, or simplified?	What can you rearrange about your idea or issue? (Resources, perspectives, starting points, sequence, etc.)
What can you substitute out? (Idea fragment, resource, concept, etc.)?	Combine ideas: What different ideas can you combine?
What analogy or metaphor can you use to explain your idea or issue?	How can you reverse your viewpoint? (Take an opposing perspective or vantage point, or use opposite of your idea or issue)
Are you solving the right problem? Is there a more significant one you're overlooking?	What sacred cow can you slay in order to promote your idea or resolve your issue?
What dissatisfaction lies behind the idea or issue? How can the irritation turn into inspiration?	We've been taught to solve problems, not recognize opportunities. Which opportunities are knocking or have been ignored?
In what ways is this idea or issue creative?	What support systems can be created or leveraged for your issue or idea?
What three factors will make it difficult to achieve your idea or solve your issue? How can you get rid of these excuses?	What fear holds you back about your idea or issue?
What motivations are behind idea or issue? What is at stake?	Have you been persistent enough? What other tactic or angle can you take to keep trying?

Source: The final 25 flashcards in the deck above were inspired or derived from Roger von Oech's 'Creative Whack Pack'.

APPENDIX E: COMMITMENT TEMPLATE

<u>PERSONAL COMMITMENTS</u>

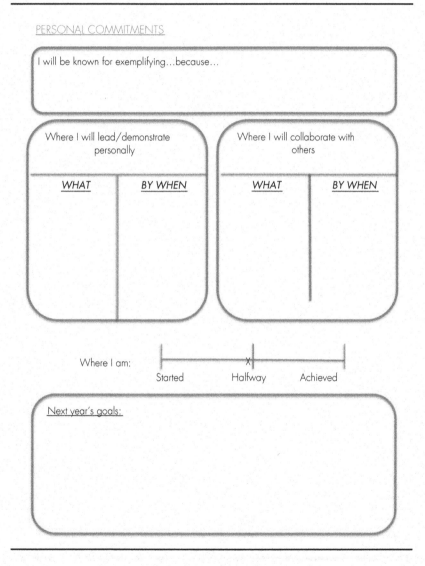

I will be known for exemplifying…because…

Where I will lead/demonstrate personally

WHAT	BY WHEN

Where I will collaborate with others

WHAT	BY WHEN

Where I am:

Started   Halfway   Achieved

<u>Next year's goals:</u>

APPENDIX F: CHANGE PRIMER

INTRODUCTION

The purpose of this Change Primer is two-fold: to explain the philosophical and conceptual background behind the approach to CHANGE in DOWE and to provide foundational knowledge and guidance to people leading change in their organization. The following explains how to maximize the positive outcomes of DOWE through CHANGE. Feel free to use this guide as a primer and/or refresher prior to any change initiative, but be sure to review this prior to the PLAN phase of the DOWE process. What's covered here is not intended to be comprehensive, nor does it prescribe the particulars of your unique initiative. These are but a fraction of extensive research, so you are encouraged to explore what's relevant to your initiative in depth.

Change initiatives live and die by their people (Shin, Taylor, & Seo, 2012, p. 727), hence the need to remain people-centered especially when it comes to the engagement, development, and use of capability in DOWE. People are the ones whose lives are impacted, and it's the people who will carry out and demonstrate the change.

Just like DESIGN, successful CHANGE ultimately boils down to curating the right combination of concepts and practices for your unique context. DOWE's CHANGE has the strength to stand on its own and the adaptability to incorporate into existing change practices if they are determined to remain in place. A word of caution, however, context changes over time, making every new change effort different *every time*. What worked in the past won't necessarily work in the future.

DESIGN enables CHANGE to happen based on in-depth knowledge of the current context and its people. Therefore, take as much care in developing customized plans for CHANGE as you did in DESIGN, for it is a serious responsibility.

PERSPECTIVES ON CHANGE

DOWE goes into change expecting people to experience some anxiety and turmoil. In the confusion that ensues, change agents and other leaders make sense of this for the organization through strategic planning, communication, and execution. That only covers what is predictable, however, so they do this knowing that no one can foresee everything. Therefore, agility is key to dealing with the unanticipated, such as unintended benefits and consequences.

"TO ASSUME THAT CHANGE IN ORGANIZATIONS IS OR CAN BE RATIONAL IS IRRATIONAL."
-W. WARNER BURKE

(Burke, 2008, p. 133)

Change disturbs established patterns of work (Choi & Ruona, 2013, citing Ford et al., 2008, p. 339), causing conflicts that are best resolved with the right interventions. For those impacted by change, it can be a personal emotional journey of highs and lows – one that everyone sees and experiences differently (Cantore & Cooperrider, 2013, p. 276). People's history with past changes also influence their perceptions (Buchanan, et al., 2003, p. 32), behaviors, and actions, for better or worse. Those with positive change experiences in the past should have that reinforced, while those who have been "emotionally scarred" have an opportunity to get their mojo back (anonymous, personal communication, February 7, 2015). Most organizations desire their employees to follow their defined path, but this isn't realistic. In cases where there is no longer alignment between the company and the individual, it is in everyone's best interest to resolve them as quickly and compassionately as possible – whether it means a re-negotiation of the social contract, a shared course correction, or an eventual parting of ways.

Like people, no two changes are alike. Each comes with their own origins and circumstances, highlighting the need for customized plans that come with practicing DOWE. At the macro level, change happens in three phases: before, during, and after. Psychologist Kurt Lewin called these unfreezing, moving, and freezing (Lewin, 1947, p. 35). *All* must be sufficiently managed in order to bring forth successful, sustainable change. (For DOWE's purposes, we've used the verbs unfreeze, change, and freeze in our terminology and before, during, and after to denote its activities.) Unfreezing aims to remove barriers, enable adaptability, and create readiness and motivation for change. What happens to people during unfreezing is not unlike what happens in transformational learning, where each person realizes the old assumptions are inadequate for making sense of the new context and therefore evolves (Courtenay, Merriam, & Reeves, 1998, pp. 77–78). Moving, according to Lewin, is "a change toward a higher level of group performance" that is a "frequently short lived... 'shot in the arm'..." (Lewin, 1958, p. 210). Once implemented, Freezing then incorporates, reinforces, and rewards the sustainability of changes (Burke, 2008, p. 104). Freezing also cements changes from one stage (or wave) to the next.

> Over the years, Lewin's use of the word "freezing" has been challenged by those who interpret it for the literal meaning of the word. They argue for "permanent slush" (Hamel & Zanini, 2014, p. 3) to reflect constant change. In reality, Lewin has been misinterpreted. In his own words, he described Freeze as "permanency for a desired period"(Lewin, 1947, p. 211). From DOWE's standpoint, Freeze doesn't describe a static state. Rather, it's about making sure changes are sufficiently established to prepare an organization for its next step and only until such point Unfreeze is needed once more.

Unfreezing, moving, and freezing are necessary phases for change initiatives. The work required for each space might be mysterious or intimidating to some. Luckily, the Burke–Litwin Causal Model of Organization

Performance and Change can be used as a guideline for the different factors at play.

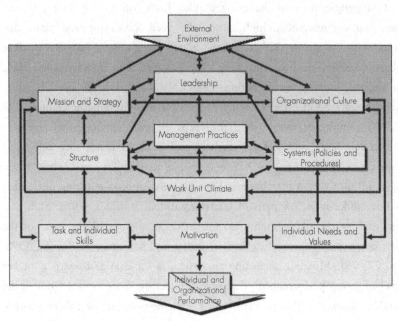

(Burke, 2008, p. 187, reprinted with permission)

This model reflects the complexity of organizational life and can be used diagnostically if desired. Each component both influences and is influenced to varying degrees because all are part of an integrated and codependent network or system. The categories or boxes in the top half of the model are called transformational factors (external environment, mission and strategy, leadership and culture). They elicit significantly different behaviors from people throughout change. The lower half represents transactional factors where change can be managed incrementally due to their operational nature (Burke, 2008, p. 189−190). While planning CHANGE, view each category as a lever. Which levers need to be pulled to realize your design? In what order? How does making changes in one category influence the other areas?

There is another dimension to consider: for each category in the Burke−Litwin Model, change occurs at different levels of the organization: the individual, team, and organization. What needs to be aligned and managed for each level to support the change? What mechanisms are at play before, during, and after change? Do roles need to be redefined or recon-firmed? How will alignment among individual, team, and organization be strengthened? The answers come from the PLAN phase of the DOWE pro-cess, as it explores and establishes the ways in which the change can be enacted through members of the organization (Choi & Ruona, 2013, citing George & Jones, 2001 and Porras & Robertson, 1992, p. 7).

Resistance to Change

There is much work to be done for Unfreeze, including: removal/ameliora-tion of barriers, enabling adaptability and resiliency, creating readiness, and motivating individuals en masse for change – all daunting tasks. However, DOWE-Rs are armed with a deep understanding of the people and context where the change will occur. This is critical for planning, because for what-ever the readiness (not only openness to change, but also the state of condi-tions and structures), there is a counterforce of resistance. It's known that the bigger the change, the bigger the potential for resistance. Those driving the change might easily see those that oppose them as wrong. However, it is never anyone's intention to ever be wrong. Oftentimes, it's the situation itself that cultivates or discourages resistance (Choi & Ruona, 2013, p. 2). This again points out the need to set the conditions in the context to support change.

Resistance can also be appropriated for the good of the change as it raises awareness, adds to the change momentum, fosters dialogue and feedback, and informs the process as a form of measurement (Choi & Ruona, 2013, p. 2). Above all else, resistance should never be taken for granted nor ignored. Knowing your organization's combination of resistance points equips you to address, leverage, minimize, and/or eliminate them altogether.

Sources of resistance are only part of what keeps the change process inter-esting and unpredictable. It includes all that is outside of your control, like people's contradictory behaviors, unintended consequences, surprises, and deviations from plans (Burke, 2008, p. 12). Like DESIGN, CHANGE is messy. Though the activities are different, the goal is the same for the organization and its people: create a sense of meaning and understanding, promote acceptance, establish a sense of control, and instill the ability to be resilient (van den Heuvel, Demerouti, Bakker, & Schaufeli, 2013, p. 14). Resilience, the ability to change, weather and recover from change (van den Heuvel, Demerouti, Bakker, & Schaufeli, 2013, p. 12), is the cure for resistance, the "restraining force moving in the direction of maintaining the status quo..." (Choi & Ruona, 2013, p. 3).

People going through change, including those taking the desired path from resistance to resilience, all go through an emotional journey. John Fisher's Personal Transition Curve illustrates its various paths, from denial, disillusionment, hostility, to moving forward.

The Process of Transition – John Fisher, 2012

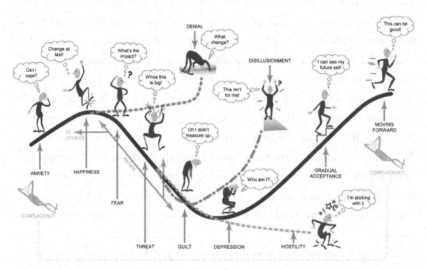

Adapted and reprinted with permission from John Fisher

Understanding the emotional journey, the breadth and complexity of change, and embracing its unpredictably is a beginning, a foundation. PLAN decides what to do about it in a way that anticipates for these and addresses them (as much as possible).

CHANGE MANAGEMENT, DOWE-STYLE

Managing change seeks to encourage readiness and resist resistance. During CHANGE, the organization's engagement and capabilities are cultivated through learning, engagement, and communication strategies working in conjunction with each other — at the individual, team, and organizational levels before, during, and after change.

Learning on All Scales

Through DOWE, an organization uses its strengths while developing new capabilities. One may wonder what learning has to do with change. The answer is *everything*. Learning, as previously discussed, is demonstrated by *changed* behavior, sustained over time, proven in observable action. The use of learning to facilitate all three phases of Lewin's model (Unfreezing, Moving, and Freezing) has been proven in practice. Learning is all about change.

People learn best when they derive meaning from an experience. They evolve when learning is so transformative that it's observable in themselves and those around them (Courtenay, Merriam, & Reeves, 1998, citing Clark, 1993, p. 65). Learning can be so profound that it is life-changing. Encountering change stimulates the human capacity to make meaning and to seek information. People search for meaning instinctively, which makes meaning-making so critical to change adaption (van den Heuvel, Demerouti, Bakker, & Schaufeli, 2013, p. 13). What better time to purposefully create more meaning and more learning opportunities than CHANGE? Fully addressing these needs increases the likelihood that you have people's under-standing and agreement to make change happen.

Learning happens in many different ways, but the opportunity is fully realized when it's supported in the right environment under the right condi-tions. Strategic planning is necessary to ensure that learning is thoughtfully structured to support the direction of the change desired, because whole sys-tems move in "the direction of what they study" (Cooperrider & Whitney, 2001, citing Whitney, 2010, p. 273).

In preparation for PLAN, let's explore learning at the organization, team, and individual levels.

Organization: Organizational Learning is about creating "collective learn-ing" as a whole (Yukl, 2009, p. 49). It's more than just scale and volume — it's about permitting knowledge to "accumulate in a manner that generates new options and possibilities" (Bartel & Garud, 2009, citing

Boland & Collopy, 2004, p. 109). Consider what needs to be done in order to create such an outcome. Strategically planned learning will sustain change through continuous growth and development in a reinforcing, virtuous cycle (Senge et al., 1999, p. 41), one where the exchange of information enhances both the organization and its employees.

Team: If learning is demonstrated by action, then the combination of two or more people exchanging actions from learning are *interactions*. Interaction, as part of the learning process, has a role to play in organizational change because "intra-team learning" has been known to "promote overall team effectiveness" (Van Der Vegt & Bunderson, 2005, p. 543) and affect meaningful change. A team that learns well together, performs well together.

Team-based learning happens when team members seek to acquire, share, refine, or connect knowledge through collaboration. This includes asking questions, challenging assumptions, seeking different perspectives, evaluating different options, and reflection (Van Der Vegt & Bunderson, 2005, citing Edmondson, 1999, 2002; Gibson & Vermeulen, 2003, p. 534). Leveraging a team's diversity also contributes to individual and group learning. Having different perspectives exposes people to new ideas and connections they wouldn't otherwise have (Van Der Vegt & Bunderson, 2005, p. 534.) Far too many organizations fail to leverage the full potential of teams, but DOWE uses PLAN to set the conditions where these behaviors and interactions multiply.

Individual: Organizations that empower individuals to learn are also recognizing the responsibility a person has for their own development (Gouillart & Kelly, 1995, p. 264). Based on what we know about learning, change, engagement, and empowerment, it is not hard to see the interplay between them: those who learn in the midst of change are more likely to be engaged, provide feedback, and contribute (Shin, Taylor, & Seo, 2012, p. 729, 740, 741), because they feel empowered and equipped to do what needs to be done (Rankinen, Suominen, Kuokkanen, Kukkurainen, and Doran, 2009, p. 405). What's learned and the speed in which it's learned varies from person to person. Planning must therefore accommodate for individuals to progressively learn at their own pace, in a reasonable period of time, asynchronously. From the onset of change, there should be multiple opportunities for individuals to increase self-awareness of emotional states and learning styles. They can decide on the learning activities that best support their individual growth throughout the change journey. This is what marketers might refer to as "personalization" in an experience.

Fueling Engagement

Organization: Even when decoupled from change, employee engagement itself is a trendy organizational topic that hasn't gone out of style. There are many definitions of employee engagement. One says that engaged employees are "those who are involved in, enthusiastic, and committed to their work and contribute to their organization in a positive manner" (O'Boyle & Harter, 2013, p. 12). Having engaged employees is obviously very desirable to employers, for they tend to be more creative, better performers, enthusiastic to help others, and lead to more satisfied stakeholders (Bakker & Daniels, 2013, p. 2). High employee engagement also equates to better business results (O'Boyle & Harter, 2013, p. 13). Using this definition and the lagging indicators that are surveys, employee engagement is often regarded as an outcome. However, it can also be a means as opposed to an end, where there's an ongoing process of interactions that result in shared obligation and positive interdependence (Saks, 2006, citing Cropanzano & Mitchell 2005, p. 614). What is employee engagement if not the result of people's interactions? According to an article in *Forbes* magazine, "The source of engagement has…everything to do with the extent to which trust, values and mission actually inspire and drive daily activities and interactions" (Seidman, 2012, p. 1). Change is another chance to leverage a set of interactions between employees and their organizations – for the better. Engaging your employees in meaningful ways not only increases engagement, but their commitment. These are critically needed for change.

That being said, the next question asked would be *how* to engage employees continuously. One way to do this is to offer a generous supply of resources that encourage adaptability, learning, and the targeted change(s). Resources play an important role in helping employees to commit, demonstrate, and implement change (Saks, 2006, p. 614). These resources include all things deemed valuable to employees that an organization can offer (Shin, Taylor, & Seo, 2012, p. 728), such as career development, training, communication, access to higher management, participation, feedback, recognition, and so on (Shin, Taylor, & Seo, 2012, p. 730). These aren't just the resources given in the past, but also those that are currently in use and those yet to be provided. Resources also include that which an organization can encourage, protect, and cultivate, such as job satisfaction (Rankinen, Suominen, Kuokkanen, Kukkurainen, & Doran, 2009, p. 405) and people's sense of psychological safety (Saks, 2006, p. 605) (more on that later). Both have been proven to increase with the use of resources as well.

Even emotional well-being and individuals' own capabilities can be regarded as resources that are especially valuable during change. This includes an employee's use of skill in new situations and their ability to weather change with resiliency (and other positive emotional states). These are personal resources to be taken into account when it comes to planning for change. Why? Individuals draw from these when they are trying to make sense of a situation (Shin, Taylor, & Seo, 2012, citing Schwarz & Clore, 2003, 2007, p. 731). Think of the differences between a resilient person (able to tackle problems or bounce back from them) versus someone feeling weak or insecure. Indeed, a threat to personal resources becomes resistance as one seeks to protect themselves. Many individuals will deal with these conflicting feelings as they seek refuge in, build, deplete, and guard their personal resources. For everyone's mutual benefit, organizations should provide the resources and conditions that build each individual's personal reserves.

At least two things can be done to accomplish this. The first is to create a sense of psychological safety, where people work according to what they believe is expected of them without fear of negative consequences (Saks, 2006, citing Kahn, 1992, p. 605). Change won't happen unless safety > threat. It's in the interest of the organization to manage change to support this bias (Shin, Taylor, & Seo, 2012, p. 731). Psychological safety can be achieved through the build up of resources that prepare people to cope, manage, and thrive throughout change (Shin, Taylor, & Seo, 2012, p. 730).

One surefire way to prove commitment to preserving psychological safety is to plan for a degree of failure (as afforded in all change). Make it not only ok, but also a vital part of the learning process. The world's most admired, innovative companies achieve this to such a degree that it is reflected in their employees' mindsets and behaviors. People usually act sad when they talk about failure and happy when they talk about wins, but the difference in affect is less extreme for an employee working at one such company. Both success and failure are opportunities, and fear of failure doesn't influence decisions. In other words, safety > threat.

The second is to offer resources proactively and in abundance, more than what is needed. Studies have shown that employees who feel ample organizational support are more likely to reciprocate with higher engagement (Saks, 2006, p. 613). When people have more than enough, their needs are met, and they might be more willing to give of themselves during change. After all, they have plenty to spare (Shin, Taylor, & Seo, 2012, p. 730). Without the inclination to protect resources, people can focus on what's important: investing in the change at hand (Shin, Taylor, & Seo, 2012, p. 741).

The deployment of resources, in its many forms, offers opportunities for employees to interact with each other and the organization, thus fulfilling the need to build employee engagement that promotes change. It's a win-win when employees feel good and the organization performs well. When managed in such a way, change creates an opportunity where people, through engagement, can draw *even closer* to the organization. DOWE-Rs, as part of the process, will identify, create, and implement the suite of resources needed to support learning, engagement, and communication for the newly designed experiences.

Team: By virtue of managing their own healthy dynamics throughout the DOWE process, the core design team should understand the building blocks of great teamwork. Now they must replicate this for others. Teams are the first place where organizational change, taking hold, can be observed. They (and their managers) are also where direction from above (the organization) and reaction from below (individuals) meet and sometimes clash. There is nothing that exposes dysfunction on any team like change. Change exposes and exacerbates poor team relations. On the other hand, teams can be a driving force for change. This is the time to re-engage teams and recontract on working norms. It's worthwhile for the organization to strengthen teams ahead of and throughout change.

Strong teams can also serve as valuable resources during change. They can be a psychologically safe place where individuals are emotionally supported during meaning/sense making. They can also be leveraged as a tool and agent of change (Higgins, Weiner, & Young, 2012, p. 369), spreading messages and implementing new ways of working. From the organizational standpoint, it is more efficient to move change in teams rather than by individual, especially since people tend to adapt to the groups they belong to

(Shin, Taylor, & Seo, 2012, p. 730). The team is also a place that encourages collaborative learning and provides the platform to practice new behaviors and capabilities.

There are at least two factors that influence a team's ability to serve in these capacities: The first is the value an individual places on being part of the team, to the degree that acceptance or belonging on the team is a motivator (Levi, 2013, p. 61). The second comes from the team's degree of cohesion – that "we-feeling" (Lewin, 1947, citing Lippett & White, 1940, 1943, p. 20) and a sense of "shared history" built over time (Van Der Vegt & Bunderson, 2005, p. 545) has to mean something to its members.

Teams can be taught to balance support of its members while holding them accountable to expectations. The team environment is where people prove their commitment to the change initiative through their behaviors and actions. Ignoring the crucial role teams play in engaging people is a gross misjudgment. Making room for this, defining it, and creating opportunities for it is part of PLAN.

Individual: Individual engagement acknowledges each person's point of view and their needs throughout change and connects them (and their contributions) to the rest of the organization. Engagement is a two-way street. It's just as important for the employee to hear as it is for the employee to be heard. Employees are often thought of collectively, as a generic group of anonymous people, and yet it is the combination of unique individuals that move change forward. Planning for individual engagement should also reflect these distinctions and provide the platform or outlets for them.

Transformative Communication

In DOWE, communication includes both the content and delivery of key information, exchanged between employees and the organization, both ways. The specifics of these are special to each DOWE initiative. However, the purpose of communication is to provide key messages needed to satisfy and encourage a dialogue of meaning throughout CHANGE. If communication does its job, people feel compelled to relinquish the status quo in favor of adopting change that promises future returns. Communication supports engagement and learning in the organization while change happens.

The content of communication should be *the source* for information related to change, both a critical resource for employees and the organization's conduit for sharing its vision of the future state. Communication fulfills employees' desire for knowledge, enables meaning making, and promotes the DOWE initiative and its changes. Its impact cannot be underestimated; language matters "because words enable worlds," as David Cooperrider says (Cantore & Cooperrider, 2013, citing Cooperrider, 1990, p. 272). If information is accessible and delivered with a combination of credibility, authenticity, and appeal, then people will likely receive and share it.

PLAN outlines the tactics to disseminate communication through multiple channels in digestible, but interconnected, pieces. Put back together, they feed into the overarching narrative, the whole story of the organization's future being co-created with its people. Narratives are the company's history in the making. Through the power of storytelling, they can share and reinforce boundaries, provide information, and inspire new ideas (Bartel & Garud, 2009, p. 108). They help people to connect and understand the differences between what has been and what is coming (Bartel & Garud, 2009, citing Van de Ven et al., 1999, p. 113–114), thus establishing continuity. Narratives evolve with the change (Bartel & Garud, 2009, p. 113), crowd-sourced through the people experiencing it. The purposefully managed narrative connects the disparate pieces together and is shared and spread throughout the organization – in teams, and to individuals – in a powerful, consistent way.

CONNECTING THE DOTS

Though discussed here separately, learning, engagement, and communication at the individual, team, and organizational levels are really one large set of highly integrated and supportive actions. Together, they enable meaning, engagement, adaptability, and resources for CHANGE. These critical links are supported by extensive research, but it's also evident how these fit together in practice. When planned in concert with one another, efficiency is achieved as these elements reinforce one another.

All activities for employees to learn, engage, and communicate are planned for ahead of change implementation in DOWE. Going in, it is critical to grasp these concepts and understand how they interact. What you plan as an organization reflects your view on this. Empower your employees to weather the emotional journey with the orchestrated resources they need to learn, engage, and communicate throughout change.

Combine all this with your deep understanding of the context and your selected design and you have the ingredients to begin the learning loops toward sustained CHANGE. It's time now to PLAN.

APPENDIX G: SAMPLE APPRECIATIVE INQUIRY (AI) SUMMIT AGENDA

SAMPLE AGENDA: APPRECIATIVE INQUIRY SUMMIT

Introduction/Kickoff
Keynote (optional)
Overview of Approach

Part I: Discover What Makes Us Great (Interactive Activities)
  Learning from each other (1:1)
  What attracted you to this organization? What keeps you here?
  When did you feel most connected to the organization?
  Discovering our resources
  Articulating our strengths

Part II: Envisioning beyond the status quo (Organizations' strengths on steroids, identification of key values, defining characteristics)
  Breakouts/World Café/Poster Board Session
  Share outs
  Provocative Propositions and Design Criteria

Part III: Design
  Build strategies from provocative propositions and criteria
  Rapid prototype possible solutions

Part IV: Planning our destiny
  Develop action plans against designs and strategies for implementation

REFERENCES

Anderson, S. (2010). $6.7 billion spent on marketing research each year. *MDX Research*, December 8. Retrieved from http://www.mdxresearch.com/6-7-billion-spent-on-marketing-research-each-year/

Armstrong, J. K. (2014). Setting a high bar. *Fast Company*, (February), 40–41.

Bailis, R. (2014). Brainstorming doesn't work – Do this instead. *Forbes.com*, October 8. Retrieved from http://www.forbes.com/sites/rochellebailis/2014/10/08/brainstorming-doesnt-work-do-this-instead/

Bakker, A. B., & Daniels, K. (2013). A day in the life of a happy worker: Introduction. In A. B. Bakker (Ed.), *A day in the life of a happy worker* (pp. 1–7). London: Psychology Press.

Bannister, D. (1962). Personal construct theory: A summary and experimental paradigm. *Acta Psychologica, 20*, 104–120.

Bartel, C. A., & Garud, R. (2009). The role of narratives in sustaining organizational innovation. *Organization Science, 20*(1), 107–117.

Battilana, J., & Casciaro, T. (2012). Change agents, networks, and institutions: A contingency theory of organizational change. *Academy of Management Journal, 55*(2), 381–398.

Baumeister, R. F., Vohs, K. D., Aaker, J. L., & Garbinsky, E. N. (2013). Some key differences between a happy life and a meaningful life. *The Journal of Positive Psychology, 8*(6), 505–516.

Beal, D. J., & Weiss, H. M. (2013). The episodic structure of life at work. In A. B. Bakker (Ed.), *A day in the life of a happy worker* (pp. 8–24). London: Psychology Press.

Benson, J., & Dresdow, S. (2013). Design thinking for assessment practice. *Journal of Management Education*, *38*(3). Retrieved from http://journals. sagepub.com/doi/abs/10.1177/1052562913507571

Bhattacharjee, A., & Mogilner, C. (2013). Happiness from ordinary and extraordinary experiences. *Journal of Consumer Research*, *41*(1), 1–17.

Briggs, R., & Stuart, G. (2006). *What sticks: Why most advertising fails and how to guarantee yours succeeds*. Chicago, IL: Kaplan Publishing.

Briley, D. A., & Aaker, J. L. (2006). Bridging the culture chasm: Ensuring that consumers are healthy, wealthy, and wise. *American Marketing Association*, *25*(1), 53–66.

Brodesser-Akner, T. (2014). Minting Julep. *Fast Company*, (February), 36–37.

Brown, S. (2014). *The Doodle revolution: Unlock the power to think differently*. New York, NY: Penguin Group.

Brown, T. (2009). *Change by design*. New York, NY: Harper Business.

Brucker, B. (2015). He was tired of looking at boring office walls, so he bought 9,000 post-it notes. The result is amazing. *Blog*, April 1. Retrieved from http://www.sunnyskyz.com/blog/766/He-Was-Tired-Of-Looking-At-Boring-Office-Walls-So-He-Bought-9-000-Post-It-Notes-The-Result-Is-Amazing

Buchanan, B., Fitzgerald, L., Ketley, D., Gollop, R., Jones, J. L., Saint Lamont, S., ... Whitby, E. (2003). No going back: A review of the literature on sustaining strategic change. *NHS Modernisation Agency*, *15*. Retrieved from http://www.qualitasconsortium.com/index.cfm/reference-material/service-transformation/no-going-back/

Buchanan, R. (1992). Wicked problems in design thinking. *Design Issues*, *8*(2).

Burke, W. W. (2008). *Organization change: Theory and practice*. Los Angeles, CA: Sage.

Cantore, S. P., & Cooperrider, D. L. (2013). Positive psychology and appreciative inquiry: The contribution of the literature to an understanding of the nature and process of change in organizations. In H. S. Leonard,

R. Lewis, & A. M. Freedman (Eds.), *The Wiley-Blackwell handbook of the psychology of leadership, change, and organizational development* (pp. 267–288). Oxford: Wiley-Blackwell.

Choi, M., & Ruona, W. E. A. (2013). Individual readiness for change. In H. S. Leonard, R. Lewis, & A. M. Freedman (Eds.), *The Wiley-Blackwell handbook of the psychology of leadership, change, and organizational development* (pp. 267–288). Oxford: Wiley-Blackwell.

Christensen, C. (2014). The 85 most disruptive ideas in our history. *Bloomberg BusinessWeek*, December 8, 44.

Chu, J. (2014). A new season at apple. *Fast Company*, February, 55.

Coelho, P. (1993). *The Alchemist*. San Francisco, CA: Harper.

Coelho, P. [@paulocoelho]. (2013). When you repeat a mistake, it is not a mistake anymore: It is a decision... [Tweet], March 1. Retrieved from https://twitter.com/paulocoelho/status/307574044037873664

Collins, J. C., & Porras, J. I. (1996). Building your company's vision. *Harvard Business Review*, 74(5), 65.

Columbia Business School Press Release. (2015, November 19). Retrieved from http://www8.gsb.columbia.edu/newsroom/newsn/3874/ceos-and-cfos-share-how-corporate-culture-matters

Cooperrider, D. L., & Whitney, D. (2001). A positive revolution in change: Appreciative inquiry. *Public Administration and Public Policy*, 87, 611–630.

Courtenay, B. C., Merriam, S. B., & Reeves, P. M. (1998). The centrality of meaning-making in transformational learning: How HIV-positive adults make sense of their lives. *Adult Education Quarterly*, 48(2), 65–84. Retrieved from http://aeq.sagepub.com/cgi/content/abstract/48/2/65

Cross, N. (2011). *Design thinking: Understanding how designers think and work*. London: Bloomsbury.

Csikszentmihalyi, M. (1991). *Flow: The psychology of optimal experience*. New York, NY: HarperPerennial. Retrieved from http://www.ode.state.or. us/opportunities/grants/nclb/title_i/a_basicprograms/schoolimprovement/transformation7flow.pdf

Das, A. S. (2011). Careers built on innovation: Lessons from PepsiCo & IBM. *Vault Blogs*, March 24. Retrieved from http://www.vault.com/blog/in-good-company-vaults-csr-blog/careers-built-on-innovation-lessons-from-pepsico-ibm

Davis, J. R., Frechette, H. M., & Boswell, E. H. (2010). *Strategic speed: Mobilize people, accelerate execution*. Boston, MA: Harvard Business Press.

De Bono, E. (1985). *Six thinking hats*. Boston, MA: Little Brown.

Epperson, J. (2013). Innovation is design and design is innovation. *Prophet.com The Inspiratory*, October 17. Retrieved from https://www.prophet.com/theinspiratory/2013/10/17/innovation-is-design-and-design-is-innovation/

Frankl, V. E. (1959). *Man's search for meaning*. Boston, MA: Beacon Press.

Fraser, H. (2013). Turning design thinking into design doing. In R. Martin & K. Christensen (Eds.), *Rotman on design: The best on design thinking from Rotman magazine* (pp. 116–121). Toronto: University of Toronto Press.

Fulmer, R. M., & Perret, S. (1993). The merlin exercise: Future by forecast or future by invention? *Journal of Management Development, 12*(6), 44–52.

Gadamer, H. (1982). *Hegel's dialectic: Five hermeneutical studies*. New Haven, CT: Yale University Press.

Garvin, D. A. (2000). *Learning in action: A guide to putting the learning organization to work*. Boston, MA: Harvard Business Press.

Gladwell, M. (2006). *The tipping point: How little things can make a big difference*. New York, NY: Little, Brown.

Gouillart, F. J., & Kelly, J. N. (1995). *Transforming the organization*. McGraw-Hill Companies.

Hamel, G., & Zanini, M. (2014). Build a change platform, not a change program. *mckinsey.com*, October. Retrieved from http://www.mckinsey.com/insights/organization/build_a_change_platform_not_a_change_program

Harris, L. C., & Ogbonna, E. (2002). The unintended consequences of culture interventions: A study of unexpected outcomes. *British Journal of Management, 13*(1), 31–49.

Haviland, W. A., Prins, H. E., McBride, B., & Walrath, D. (2013). *Cultural anthropology: The human challenge.* Boston, MA: Cengage Learning.

Higgins, M. C., Weiner, J., & Young, L. (2012). Implementation teams: A new lever for organizational change. *Journal of Organizational Behavior, 33*(3), 366–388.

Insight [Defs. 1 & 2]. (n.d.). *dictionary.com.* Retrieved from http://www.dictionary.com/browse/insight?s=t

Johnson, S. (2010). *Where good ideas come from: The natural history of innovation.* New York, NY: Riverhead Books.

Johnson, S. (2014). Why inventors misjudge how we'll abuse their creations. *wired.com*, October 15. Retrieved from http://www.wired.com/2014/10/technological-innovation-oversights/

Kabat-Zinn, J. (1991). *Full catastrophe living: Using the wisdom of your body and mind to face stress, pain, and illness.* New York, NY: Dell Publishing Group.

Keeley, L., Walters, H., Pikkel, R., & Quinn, B. (2013). *Ten types of innovation: The discipline of building breakthroughs.* Hoboken, NJ: John Wiley & Sons.

Kelley, T. (2005). *The ten faces of innovation: IDEO's strategies for beating the devil's advocate & driving creativity throughout your organization.* New York, NY: Currency Doubleday.

Kensing, F., & Blomberg, J. (1998). Participatory design: Issues and concerns. *Computer Supported Cooperative Work (CSCW), 7*(3–4), 167–185.

Kolko, J. (2010). Abductive thinking and sensemaking: The drivers of design Synthesis. *MIT's Design Issues, 26*(1), 15–28. Retrieved from http://www.jonkolko.com/writingAbductiveThinking.php. Accessed on September12, 2017.

Kolko, J. (2011). *Exposing the magic of design: A practitioner's guide to the methods and theory of synthesis.* Oxford: Oxford University Press.

Krishna, G. (2015). *The best interface is no interface.* San Francisco, CA: Peachpit.

Krum, R. (2014). *Cool infographics: Effective communication with data visualization and design.* Hoboken, NJ: John Wiley & Sons.

Kumar, V. (2013). *101 design methods: A structured approach for driving innovation in your organization*. Hoboken, NJ: John Wiley & Sons.

LaClair, J. A., & Rao, R. P. (2002). Helping employees embrace change. *mckinsey.com*, November. Retrieved from https://www.mckinsey.com/business-functions/organization/our-insights/helping-employees-embrace-change

Lamott, A. (1994). *Bird by bird: Some instructions on writing and life*. New York, NY: Anchor.

Lawson, M., & Barrow, J. (2014). *Human walking program* [video file], November 17. Retrieved from https://vimeo.com/112130729

Leahey, C. (2012). Angela Ahrendts: The secrets behind Burberry's growth. *Fortune.com*, June 19. Retrieved from http://fortune.com/2012/06/19/angela-ahrendts-the-secrets-behind-burberrys-growth/

Levi, D. (2013). *Group dynamics for teams*. Los Angeles, CA: Sage Publications.

Lewin, K. (1947). Frontiers in group dynamics: Concept, method and reality in social science, social equilibria and social change. *Human Relations, 1*(1), 5–41. doi:10.1177/001872674700100103. Retrieved from http://hum.sagepub.com/content/1/1/5

Lewin, K. (1958). Group decision and social change. In E. E. Maccoby, T. M. Newcomb, & E. L. Hartley (Eds.), *Readings in social psychology* (pp. 197–211). New York, NY: Henry Holt and Company.

Lewis, T. (2015). *The neuroscience of love*. Speech presented at Wonderfest, Oshman Family JCC, Palo Alto, CA, August 4.

Liedkta, L., & Olgilvie, T. (2011). *Designing for growth: A design thinking tool kit for managers*. New York, NY: Columbia University Press.

Liedtka, J. (2013, Fall). *Kinds of problems for design thinking*. Lecture, Design Thinking for Innovation Online Course, University of Virginia.

Madsbjerg, C., & Rasmussen, M. B. (2014). *The moment of clarity: Using the human sciences to solve your toughest business problems*. Boston, MA: Harvard Business Review Press.

Madson, P. R. (2005). *Improv wisdom: Don't prepare, just show up*. New York, NY: Bell Tower.

Manjoo, F. (2012). This is the greatest hoodie ever made. *Slate.com*, December 4. Retrieved from http://www.slate.com/articles/technology/technology/2012/12/american_giant_hoodie_this_is_the_greatest_sweatshirt_known_to_man.single.html

Marsick, V. J., Sauquet, A., & Yorks, L. (2006). Learning through reflection. In M. Deutsch, P. T. Coleman, & E. C. Marcus (Eds.), *The handbook of conflict resolution: Theory and practice* (pp. 486–506). San Francisco, CA: Jossey-Bass.

McCracken, G. (2009). *Chief culture officer: How to create a living breathing, corporation.* New York, NY: Basic Books.

Mullen, B., Johnson, C., & Salas, E. (1991). Productivity loss in brainstorming groups: A meta-analytic integration. *Basic and Applied Social Psychology, 12*(1), 3–23.

Newman, J. (2014). To Siri, With Love: How one boy with autism became B.F.F.'s with Apple's Siri. *The New York Times*, October 17. Retrieved from http://nyti.ms/1y0lvAu

Norton, M. I., Mochon, D., & Ariely, D. (2012). The IKEA effect: When labor leads to love. *Journal of Consumer Psychology, 22*(3), 453–460.

O'Boyle, E., & Harter, J. (2013). *State of the American workplace: Employee engagement insights for US business leaders.* Washington, DC: Gallup.

O'Toole, J. (1995). *Leading change: Overcoming the ideology of comfort and the tyranny of custom.* San Francisco, CA: Jossey-Bass, A Wiley Imprint.

Pink, D. H. (2005). *A whole new mind: Why right-brainers will rule the future.* New York, NY: Riverhead Books/The Penguin Group.

Pothukuchi, V., Damanpour, F., Choi, J., Chen, C. C., & Park, S. H. (2002). National and organizational culture differences and international joint venture performance. *Journal of International Business Studies, 33*(2), 243–265.

Prud'homme van Reine, P. (2017). The culture of design thinking for innovation. *Journal of Innovation Management, 5*(2), 56–80.

Putnam, L. L., Myers, K. K., & Gailliard, B. M. (2013). Examining the tensions in workplace flexibility and exploring options for new directions. *Human Relations*, 67(4), 413–440.

Rankinen, S., Suominen, T., Kuokkanen, L., Kukkurainen, M. L., & Doran, D. (2009). Work empowerment in multidisciplinary teams during organizational change. *International Journal of Nursing Practice*, 15(5), 403–416.

Rockwell, N. (1988). *My adventures as an illustrator*. Stockbridge, MA: The Norman Rockwell Museum.

Rose, C. (2014). Charlie Rose talks to Tory Burch. *Bloomberg Business Week*, October 16. Retrieved from http://www.bloomberg.com/bw/articles/2014-10-16/tory-burch-on-ambition-gender-pay-gap-and-rising-to-the-occasion

Ruch, D. (2016). What to do when you can no longer afford those flashy office perks. *FastCompany.com*, January 29. Retrieved from http://www.fastcompany.com/3056017/the-future-of-work/what-to-do-when-you-can-no-longer-afford-those-flashy-office-perks

Sacks, D. (2014). Fixing this one big problem helped turn around struggling furniture retailer West Elm. *Fast Company*, April. Retrieved from http://www.fastcompany.com/3026993/the-future-of-furniture-west-elm

Saks, A. M. (2006). Antecedents and consequences of employee engagement. *Journal of Managerial Psychology*, 21(7), 600–619.

Sale, J. E., Lohfeld, L. H., & Brazil, F. K. (2002). Revisiting the quantitative-qualitative debate: Implications for mixed-methods research. *Quality and Quantity*, 36(1), 43–53.

Schein, E. (2017). *Organizational culture and leadership*. Hoboken, NJ: John Wiley & Sons.

Schmitt, B. H. (2010). *Customer experience management: A revolutionary approach to connecting with your customers*. Hoboken, NJ: John Wiley & Sons.

Schumacher, E. F. (1994). Good work. In C. Whitmyer (Ed.), *Mindfulness and meaningful work: Explorations in right livelihood*. Berkeley, CA: Parallax Press.

Schwartz, B., Ward, A., Monterosso, J., Lyubomirsky, S., White, K., & Lehman, D. R. (2002). Maximizing versus satisficing: Happiness is a matter of choice. *Journal of Personality and Social Psychology, 83*(5), 1178–1197.

Seidman, D. (2012). (Almost) Everything we think about employee engagement is wrong. *Forbes.com*, September. Retrieved from https://www.forbes.com/sites/dovseidman/2012/09/20/everything-we-think-about-employee-engagement-is-wrong/

Senge, P., Kleiner, A., Roberts, C., Ross, R., Roth, G., & Smith, B. (1999). *The dance of change: The challenges to sustaining momentum in learning organizations.* New York, NY: Currency Doubleday.

Senge, P. N. (2006). *The fifth discipline: The art and practice of the learning organization.* New York, NY: Doubleday.

Shin, J., Taylor, M. S., & Seo, M. G. (2012). Resources for change: The relationships of organizational inducements and psychological resilience to employees' attitudes and behaviors toward organizational change. *Academy of Management Journal, 55*(3), 727–748.

Shockley, K. M., Thompson, C. A., & Andreassi, J. K. (2013). Workplace culture and work-life integration. In D. A. Major & R. J. Burke (Eds.), *Handbook of work–life integration among professionals: Challenges and opportunities* (pp. 310–333). Cheltenham: Edward Elgar Publishing.

Solis, B. (2013). *[What's the future] of business? Changing the way businesses create experiences.* Hoboken, NJ: John Wiley & Sons.

Stanford University d.school. (2009). d.school brainstorming rules [video file], July 13. Retrieved from https://www.youtube.com/watch?v=W1h5L_0rFz8

Stanford University d.school. *How to assume a beginners mindset* [PowerPoint File]. Retrieved from Mindset https://dschool-old.stanford.edu/groups/k12/wiki/4e22d/Beginners_mind.html. Accessed on August 6, 2010.

Stanford University d.school's Bootcamp Bootleg. (2009). Retrieved from https://dschool.stanford.edu/resources/the-bootcamp-bootleg

Stelter, B. (2014). Inside the ouster of the 'Today' Show Boss. *CNN Money*, November 19. Retrieved from http://money.cnn.com/2014/11/18/media/today-show-tick-tock/index.html?hpt=hp_t4

Stenham, P., Garvey, G., Rojo, T., Turnage, M., Dangerfield, F., Wainright, M., ... McGregor, W. (2012). Top artists reveal how to find creative inspiration. *The Guardian*, January 2. Retrieved from http://www.theguardian.com/culture/2012/jan/02/top-artists-creative-inspiration

Sull, D., Homkes, R., & Sull, C. (2015). Why strategy execution unravels—and what to do about it. *Harvard Business Review*, March. Retrieved from https://hbr.org/2015/03/why-strategy-execution-unravelsand-what-to-do-about-it

Tapscott, S., & Williams, A. (2007). Innovation in the age of mass collaboration. *BloombergBusiness*, February 1. Retrieved from http://www.bloomberg.com/bw/stories/2007-02-01/innovation-in-the-age-of-mass-collaborationbusinessweek-business-news-stock-market-and-financial-advice

The Nerd Machine. (2013). Conversation with Tom Hiddleston [video file], July 21. Retrieved from https://www.youtube.com/watch?v=jLX-tdqEjUg

The RSA. (2013). Brene Brown on empathy [video file], December 10. Retrieved from https://www.youtube.com/watch?v=1Evwgu369Jw

The RSA. (2015). Brene Brown on blame [video file], February 3. Retrieved from https://www.youtube.com/watch?v=RZWf2_2L2v8

The Today Show. (2015). Pete Carroll's full interview with Matt Lauer [video file], February 5. Retrieved from http://www.today.com/video/today/56934537

Thrift: We're Giving Away Code. (2007 April 1). Retrieved from https://www.facebook.com/notes/facebook/thrift-were-giving-away-code/2261927130

Tuckman, B. W. (1965). Developmental sequence in small groups. *Psychological Bulletin*, 63(6), 384–399. Retrieved from http://web.mit.edu/curhan/www/docs/Articles/15341_Readings/Group_Dynamics/Tuckman_1965_Developmental_sequence_in_small_groups.pdf

van den Heuvel, M., Demerouti, E., Bakker, A. B., & Schaufeli, W. B. (2013). Adapting to Change: The value of change information and meaning-making. *Journal of Vocational Behavior*, 83(1), 11–21.

Van Der Vegt, G. S., & Bunderson, J. S. (2005). Learning and performance in multidisciplinary teams: The importance of collective team identification. *Academy of Management Journal*, 48(3), 532–547.

von Oech, R. (2003). *Roger von Oech's creative whack pack: 64 creative strategies to provoke and inspire your thinking*. Stamford, CT: U.S. Game Systems, Inc.

von Oech, R. (2008). *A whack on the side of the head: How you can be more creative*. New York, NY: Business Plus.

Williams, S., & Perez, M. (2014). Yahoo's acquisition strategy is actually a talent strategy. *WashingtonPost.com*, July 6. Retrieved from http://www.washingtonpost.com/business/capitalbusiness/yahoos-acquisition-strategy-is-actually-a-talent-strategy/2014/07/03/d8bb72fc-0070-11e4-8fd0-3a663dfa68ac_story.html

Wiseman, T. (1996). A concept analysis of empathy. *Journal of Advanced Nursing, 23*(6), 1162–1167.

Wujec, T. (2010). Build a tower, build a team [video file], February. Retrieved from https://www.ted.com/talks/tom_wujec_build_a_tower#t-136902

Xanthopoulou, D., & Bakker, A. B. (2013). State work engagement: The significance of within-person fluctuations. In A. Bakker (Ed.), *A day in the life of a happy worker*. London: Psychology Press.

Yukl, G. (2009). Leading organizational learning: Reflections on theory and research. *The Leadership Quarterly, 20*(1), 49–53.

Zax, D. (2012). Square's director of experience on why an in-house Barista makes everyone happy. *Fast Company*, December 13. Retrieved from http://www.fastcompany.com/3003932/squares-director-experience-why-house-barista-makes-everyone-happy

INDEX